Landmark Visitors Guide

Rhc

Brian & Eilee~ ~rson

Published by
Landmark Publishing
Ashbourne Hall, Cokayne Ave, Ashbourne,
Derbyshire DE6 1EJ England

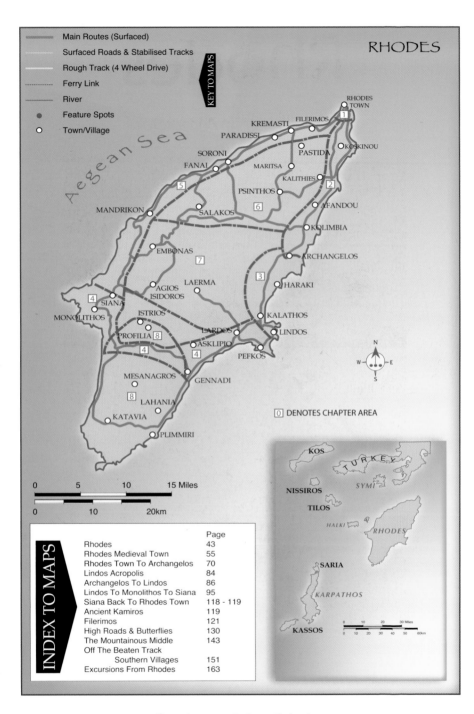

Opposite page: Anthony Quinn bay

Landmark Visitors Guide

Rhodes

Brian & Eileen Anderson

Contents

Contents

Introduction

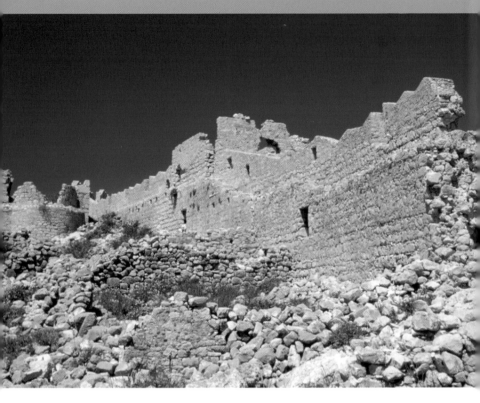

Beyond the glittering array of tall, slender masts of luxurious yachts in Mandraki harbour lie the sturdy medieval walls of Rhodes old town. No mere relic of the past, the old town houses a thriving community which bustles with activity, tourist shops, tavernas, bars, houses and even hotels. This is the heartbeat of Rhodes town in the eyes of the tourist, but the commercial heart beats in the modern city lying outside the old town walls. Ancient and modern, this is Rhodes, an island which borrows incessantly from the passing of time whilst relinquishing nothing. An island where harmony reigns between the old and the new, where a sophisticated north rubs shoulders with a rural south.

Above: Halki, castle of the Knights of St John

Rhodes by name: Sunshine or Roses by Nature?

There are plenty of theories on how Rhodes, or Rodos in Greek, earned its name but no great certainty. One of the least attractive relates to snakes. In antiquity the island was infested with them so the name may have derived from an old Phoenician word, jarod or erod, meaning snake. According to legend, it was to eradicate snakes that the ancients introduced the deer. On a more appealing theme, Rodos may have been born from the Greek word rodon meaning rose (triandafyllo is now more commonly used). It would be convincing if Rhodes was renowned for its roses in antiquity but it is not especially, except for rock roses which are abundant on the island. Also common on the island are roidon, or pomegranate, and this is a strongly favoured contender by some.

The Greeks might have invented logic but they are romantics at heart and have always been quick to cast facts aside for a good myth. Forget all the theories and just look back into deep history. Zeus overlooked the sun god Helios when assigning islands. Fortunately, a new island rose from the sea which solved the problem. This was given to Helios who then took up residence with his intended, Rodos, named the island after her and gifted it with perpetual sunshine.

Just to add to the confusion, archaeologists have turned up some old Rhodian coins with the head of the sun god Helios on one side and a flower, thought to be a pomegranate, on the other.

Its shoreline is its playground enjoyed by the Greeks and visitors alike. Sandy beaches, shingle beaches, large beaches, small beaches, busy beaches, quiet beaches, Rhodes has them all. Water sports in variety with activities to meet every need but if its just a restful sunbed in the shadow of a giant umbrella in striking distance of a bar, it will not be difficult to find. When the cultural appetite grows there is plenty of sustenance around; three ancient cities await, Lindos, Kamiros and Ialysos, medieval castles in Rhodes town and Monolithos, and countryside excursions to the Valley of the Butterflies, to the seven springs, Efta Pigis or to the top of the second highest mountain on the island, Profitis Ilias.

The following chapters are presented as tours, not just through the landscape but through history, culture and sometimes the natural history, to reveal the facets of Rhodes which drew hordes of invaders in the past and still does in the guise of tourism. The first chapter takes Rhodes Town by storm while the next four leisurely tour adjacent sections around the perimeter of the island which, taken together, offer a complete round-the-island tour. Inland Rhodes is not forgotten with three chapters devoted to all the small inland villages where an old lifestyle is still to be found. For those intent on trying an offshore excursion, the final chapter is there to enrich the experience.

PEOPLE & CULTURE

In spite of the island's turbulent history and the parade of masters over the centuries, the people of Rhodes have never lost their Greekness. Their conviviality and hospitality to strangers wins the island many friends. Sadly, these qualities are subdued by the pressure of work in the height of the tourist season but never squashed. Away from all the bustle, it takes only a cheerful greeting, sometimes only a smile, to be on the receiving end of their hospitality. It may take the form of an orange pulled from a bag or a handful of freshly grown broad beans but whatever it is, it is considered bad manners to refuse. Language barriers do not exist for the Greeks and mostly they will chatter away in their native tongue in the full expectancy that you will understand some or part of whatever they are saying. Body language and gesticulations play a full part too. The head is frequently used this way. Assent is signified by

a slight nod to the side and no is indicted by a slight toss of the head upward often accompanied by a slight 'tchh' sound. If words fail, an invitation to come or to follow is mostly by a downward pawing movement of the hand. If this is an invitation into the home, the first offering will be some sweet preserves served with a glass of water. To refuse this is to refuse their hospitality but it is not essential to eat all of it. No matter how poor the hosts, any suggestion of payment will cause deep offence but a small present for a child would be acceptable. The surprise arrival of a bottle of wine or ouzo on your table in the taverna may well be the gift of a new acquaintance. The custom here is to pour a glass to toast the sender and drink at least a little of the bottle but there will be no expectation that it is all consumed. The penetration of polite conversation often takes visitors by surprise. After the usual health enquiries, which are taken seriously by the Greeks, the conversation quickly moves into questions about the family, how many sons, daughters and their ages. Unreserved admiration is expressed for parents of large families especially with many sons. From this point enquiries continue about work and will invariably contain a question which throws unprepared visitors almost into a state of shock: 'How much do you earn?' In Greek society it would be considered impolite not to ask.

The family unit is strong and still the basis of Greek society, although there are signs that the bonds are starting to weaken under western influences. It is sons who receive the adulation and are totally spoilt by their parents. This does not mean that daughters are not welcomed, as in some societies, and the ideal family is regarded as one son and one daughter. It is remarkable just how many Greek families comprise just two children. Parental influence is not as strong as it used to be when the time is right for their children to marry. Western influences are more and more apparent with couples living together before marriage. It used to be the duty of the son to stand by his parents to ensure that suitable matches are made for all his sisters before he can contemplate marriage. Although a dowry is no longer a legal requirement, and this repeal was only in recent times, it is still perpetuated in some families. A girl goes into marriage often with the gift of a furnished house or apartment from her parents. It remains the girl's property and her security. In the same way gifts of gold to the bride, also to provide for her security, are not unusual. At least the newly wedded couple start life without the burden of debt and are able to build and plan a future for their own children. The family unit extends into business too. The Greek preference is for self employment, failing that a secure job with the state, and most of the small businesses employ only family which are eventually passed down via sons and daughters.

It is a male dominated society in which it is demeaning for a man to indulge in women's tasks. This distinct role division is ingrained into society and a woman would lose face if her man was seen sweeping floors or washing dishes. Attitudes are slowly changing amongst the younger generation. The segregation of the sexes too is inbuilt into society. When family or friends enjoy a meal in a taverna, which can be quite a boisterous affair, there is usually a polarisation where the men cluster to one end of the table and the women to the other. Until recently, only men had the freedom to go out alone and it still is not uncommon to see all-male groups in tavernas or bars. Again signs of change are evident even in this area and young women are becoming part of the social scene. Mixed groups of young people out enjoying themselves no longer raises eyebrows as it would have done a couple of decades ago.

The role of women in the broader society has been recognised in legislation. They acquired the vote only in 1952 and the first woman Deputy was elected to Parliament the following year. Sexual discrimination in career opportunities and in the place of work has been outlawed. Many practical steps have been taken to assist the integration of women as equals in society. Low cost nurseries providing child places have been provided to free women to work and they have acquired rights of ownership after marriage and an equal share of communal property on divorce. Women now hold important posts in all branches of the Civil Service and in commerce but, in spite of all their progress, equality is only

Right: Portrait painter at work by the entrance to Rhodes old town
Below: Kiki, one of the union of portrait painters

accepted in the big cities. Throughout rural Greece it remains contrary to the culture and fundamental change will only be fully accepted very slowly. For women travelling alone in Greece there are no exceptional problems. The incidence of violent crime, including rape, is much lower than in other western societies. But it is not unknown, especially in Faliraki, and wariness of possible situations should be observed. Greek men firmly believe that they are irresistible to all women so their attentions can be expected. Rhodes is very cosmopolitan and women alone in bars or tavernas are an accepted part of the scenery.

GEOGRAPHY & TOPOGRAPHY

Rhodes is the largest island of the Dodecanese group which lies in the south east Aegean Sea scrambled around the coast of Asia Minor. Dodecanese translates to twelve islands but there are normally fourteen assigned to this group as well as some forty uninhabited islets. In shape Rhodes resembles an almond with the symmetry spoilt only by opposing headlands. Its 84km (52 miles) length lies on a north east-south west axis with the northern end approaching to within 11km (7 mile) of the Turkish coastline whilst the widest distance, 35km (28 mile), is measured between Cape Mitias in the east and Cape Armenistos in the west.

Along with Crete and Karpathos, Rhodes is regarded as part of the 'Cretan arc', the land which once linked the Peloponnese with Asia Minor. Tectonic plate movements and upheavals in Tertiary times left only the summits of a mountain chain visible above sea level. which are now these islands. The arc forms the southern boundary of the Aegean and separates it from the Mediterranean. Thus the west coast of Rhodes borders the Aegean sea whilst the east coast bathes in the Mediterranean.

Much of the central part of the island is hilly but there are only two regions of significantly high ground. Mount Ataviros, a large, barren mass of grey rock overlooking the village of Embonas, is the highest standing at an elevation of 1215m/4000ft. Its steep slopes make it look inaccessible but ascent on foot is easily accomplished by experienced walkers. The other region, Mount Profitis Ilias, lies north of this and, at 900m/2960ft, is appreciably lower and well covered by vegetation. The central upland area gathers abundant winter rainfall and is well furnished with rivers and streams. Many of these rage in winter, especially after storms, and cut out wide beds at the lower levels but few are perennial.

Land suitable for cultivation is scattered in pockets around the island, some of it reclaimed from the hillsides by the use of terracing. None of the areas, except perhaps those in the south east, are large enough to be intensively farmed by modern methods and equipment.

11

POLITICS

Politics is an overriding obsession with the Greeks. Free political expression arrived only in 1974 with the fall of the dictatorship. All the three hundred seats in the single chamber parliament are filled by parties formed after 1974. Essentially a two party system is evolving with the contestants being the socialist PASOK, the Panhellenic Socialist Movement and the New Democracy party (ND) with conservative leanings. Not without some support is the Communist Party of Greece, the KKE. All these symbols are liberally painted on bridges and buildings throughout the country. After years of socialist rule, the New Democracy under Mitsotakis held the balance of power by the slenderest of margins, one seat, for a time but the elections of 1993 saw the control swing back to PASOK led by the ageing Papandreou. The political system is slowly maturing but it still faces some serious problems in bureaucracy, nepotism, petty corruption, low productivity and poor social services. Greece's membership of the EEC has itself been a stabilising influence and the country has benefited greatly from grants, enormous loans and subsidies over recent years. A stabilisation programme imposed from Brussels is currently in place trying to reduce government spending and bring inflation under control. Regardless of which party holds the balance of power, strikes are a way of life in Greece and barely a week passes without some

sector providing the action. It does occasionally become a serious problem for the traveller when the action moves into a concerted phase and banks, transport and tavernas, for example, all co-ordinate their strikes.

For the Greeks, politics is a passion akin to football and demands the same loyalty. The uncommitted or floating voter is a rare species. Prime time Saturday evening television is often filled with two hours of political debate which is avidly followed even in the tavernas. Visitors may not escape being drawn into political discussion and are likely to be tested on two main topics; relations between Greece and Turkey and the Cyprus question.

ECONOMY

Tourism now plays a leading role and over the past decade it has given a considerable boost to the building industry with the demand for hotels, apartments, restaurants and bars, to road construction and to the service sector in general. Tourism is easily the major earner of hard currency.

Outside tourism, agriculture still remains important and involves many of the islanders even though they may have other employment. This is largely a consequence of the dowry and inheritance laws which sees the land constantly divided into small parcels. Land sales or bartering within a family will sometimes coalesce adjoining plots but customs in general keep the plots well divided and ensure that virtually every Rhodian has land to farm. It also makes the application of modern farming methods with big machinery impractical. Grain, especially wheat, is a major crop but quick maturing barley is grown in winter as a feed crop and red oats in summer.

Fruits are important too and there is none more important than the olive. Citrus fruits are also popular and extensive orange groves are seen around Massari and Malona. It is along the main road here that orange vendors pitch their stalls through the early part of the season to catch the passing trade. The vine too is extensively grown for the island's wine (see the feature on wine tasting p.139) and the favoured locations are on the cooler side of the island around Embonas. Two other specialities of Rhodes are melons and water melons which can be seen growing in the fields down in the south of the island, especially around Apolakia.

Fishing remains a small but important sector and tourism has helped to sustain it. The fleet is nothing more than an armada of small boats based in the coastal villages around the island. Even Faliraki, a major tourist resort, still has a small bay where fishing boats anchor.

Cottage industries, especially pottery, have flourished under tourism. Keramik factories litter the highways always with large car parks to accommodate coaches and most tourist shops sell some pottery. Hand made carpets, a feature of the island just a decade ago, have declined in importance but are still to be seen in the shops.

LAW & ORDER

The incidence of violent crime, rape, theft and robbery is still far lower than in most other western cultures but not absent. Although sensible precautions are always advisable, it is not something that need concern the tourist too much. It still pays to be sensible with personal property, especially cameras, and protect it as at home. It is said that most of the petty thievery arrives and leaves with the visitors but with plenty of Albanians around now, they too are shouldering some of the blame. Generally, the Greeks have their own moral code for living in which there are some distinctly eastern traits and ambiguities. They have a basic honesty which means that if you leave your change in their shop then they will chase down the street after you to return it. On the other hand, the same owner may well have twisted you out of a euro or two by quoting a wrong price. This is regarded as smart and foreigners are fair game. Their attitude to the laws in general are not always easy to comprehend. There are many laws which the public just totally and completely ignore. Parking is one of them. It is hard to find a parking space even where a street is littered with no parking signs. Periodically the police come along with parking tickets but few ever get paid for various reasons so the parking continues. It is the same

13

with safety belts in cars. The law is very explicit on this, safety belts are compulsory but drivers rarely wear them. Every few months there is an announcement that the fine is to be increased for this offence and that there will be a check in a few days time. On the day of the check seat belts are worn and on the following day everything reverts to as it was. There is also a law that motorcyclists should wear crash helmets but many motorcyclists still do not wear them and bikes for hire are not always offered with crash helmets. Disobedience of these driving laws is visible, it can be observed every day of the week but the same philosophy applies to many laws in every day life.

RELIGION

The Orthodox Church is firmly established and dominates the religious scene. Other denominations are tolerated but proselytisation is not. The Church of Rhodes and the Dodecanese is an autonomous institution and is not controlled by the church of the Greek mainland but owes its allegiance directly to the Ecumenical Patriarch of Constantinople. Head of the church is Metropolitan Bishop of Rhodes and included within the diocese are the islands of Halki, Simi, Tilos and Nisyros.

Priests move about the community in their black ankle-length cassocks, black hat and full beard. They may be seen drinking coffee in the kafenion and travelling by bus when, more than likely, someone will spring up to offer a seat but they are rigidly church based without the role of social worker in the wider community. As in many other western cultures, the church is slowly losing its power amongst the people, especially the younger generation. The acceptance of civil marriage was forced on the church by the government following reforms in 1981. Up until

that time, Greeks married abroad by civil ceremony were not accepted as married under the Government's own civil law. Abortion too was legalised, also against church opposition, but this did nothing more than legalise the existing high rate of abortion. It has long been used as a means of family planning. The Church still controls

14

Above: One of the Papas, not an uncommon sight on Rhodes

a lot of agricultural land and unused land which the government is trying to wrestle away to put into the hands of farmers and co-operatives.

On high days and holy days, and there are many in the Greek calendar, the church comes into its own and, for a brief time becomes the focus of community life. Easter is the most important event of the year and this and other religious events are discussed in the Fact File. The church played an important role throughout the Byzantine years as guardian of the Greek culture. It organised secret schools to educate the children and preserve the language.

FOLK ART

Folk art on Rhodes is very distinctive. Pottery, textiles, woodwork and other expressions of folk art tend to be very traditional and conservative in design. Designs and techniques are handed down from generation to generation with little change or

Fast Food Greek Style

The Greeks are great nibblers, particularly in the mornings, so there is no shortage of fast-food. 'Pies' with various fillings, usually made with filo pastry and looking like a Cornish pasty:-

Tiropitta: cheese.

Spanakopitta: spinach only or with cheese and eggs.

Kreatopitta: minced meat.

also available:

Pizza, either mini size or in slices

Souvlaki: small pieces of meat on a wooden skewer served with a lump of bread or with pitta. *Doner me pitta*: slices of meat from the 'gyros' (meat cooked on a vertical spit) placed in a pitta parcel with a little yoghurt, tomato and onion.

Tost: usually a slice of ham and cheese toasted between unbuttered bread.

Koulouria - Sesame seed encrusted rings are available from bread shops.

and for the sweet tooth:-

Milopitta: apple pie.

Bougatza: vanilla custard pie.

Freshly pressed orange juice is widely available.

evolution. As in any poor society, the object must also fulfil a function even though it may be decoratively coloured or crafted. Decorative pottery is made throughout the island and is characterised by its vivid coloration with reds, greens and blues. Plates on Rhodes had a special place in the traditional home for decoration and as a display of wealth. Work aimed specifically for the tourist market relies heavily on designs from early history or from Greek mythology. Woven and embroidered textiles are also commonly found throughout the island. Embroidery has proved popular with visitors and it is not uncommon for village ladies to arrange displays along the roadside of tourist trails, especially at Lindos. Museums of folk art are becoming increasingly popular, like the ones at Apollona, Asklipio, Embona and Kritinia which are interesting for their displays of national costumes and household and farming implements.

FOOD & DRINK

Eating out in Greece, traditionally inexpensive, is a national pastime but even that is under threat with rising prices and high rates of inflation. It was unthinkable for a Greek family to entertain friends or family to a meal at home. As a party they would head for the taverna and the host would collect the bill. Not only was the taverna a place to eat but it was also a place of entertainment. After the meal, tables would be pushed back, the owner would produce a bouzouki or similar instrument and the menfolk would rise to dance. Perhaps later the women might join the dancing too. Sadly this now happens only on festive occasions. Gone is the bouzouki to be replaced by the television and the atmosphere of the taverna is generally more subdued. Watching the Greeks eat is a pleasure in itself. Seldom do they order individually, instead they order a vast number of communal dishes which fill the table to overflowing. There is no rush to eat the food either, conversation continues at a high pitch whilst the diners pick and nibble their way steadily through the dishes. They are far less concerned about cold food and many dishes which arrive hot are cold before they are eaten. Some tourists find it a bit disconcerting when their meals are actually served on the cool side but, in most tourist areas, the message that tourists generally like their food hot has registered.

Although the Greek cuisine is quite extensive, tavernas tend only to have a limited menu. Lunch time, between 2 and 3 o'clock after work finishes, is the only meal of the day for which the chef will prepare a range of cooked dishes. For the evening trade, and the Greeks are notoriously late eaters, the menu offers whatever is left over from lunch, which has often been kept warm for hours, and a range of grills which are cooked to order. Charcoal is generally used for grilling and it is not unusual to see large charcoal grills by the doorway or outside in summer. Although the tavernas are the traditional eating places, Rhodes town has a selection of restaurants which provide a better standard of decor in particular and offer a more international cuisine.

Tavernas are obliged to have a menu but many still do not. Instead diners will be shown a glass show case exhibiting the range of dishes available or, and this is still very common in the villages, they will be led into the kitchen to see exactly what is cooking. If difficulties are experienced in the final choice then spoons may appear for a tasting session. In an effort to improve standards, a government decree instructs that all tables should have a cloth table cloth. Previously it was usual just to have a plain piece of polythene which was changed for each new client. It served a double purpose because at the end of the meal all scraps from the plates would be tipped into it and the whole lot bundled up and removed. Now the situation has changed. Tables are fitted with a decorative table cloth but this is securely protected by a polythene sheet covered by paper square and only the latter is laid fresh each time. Should there be a menu on the table then it will probably be in Greek and English but it will only show a partial correspondence with the dishes on offer since seasonal foods are often not listed so it still pays to ask. It is unusual to find the table laid, apart from the oil and vinegar flasks, paper napkins and the inevitable toothpicks, but the cutlery arrives with bread after an order is placed.

There is no special form in a taverna and no conventions to follow. The Greeks often go in for a plate of chips and a beer and make it last half the night. For diners though, it is usual to begin with one or a selection of the starters or mezedes on offer. These include *tzatsiki* (a yoghurt, cucumber and garlic dip), *taramasalata* (fish roe mixed with potato, oil and vinegar, the pinker the better), *melitzano salata* (an aubergine dip with tomato and garlic) and *humus*, another dip this time from chick-peas. Fresh vegetables are rarely available but two vegetables which turn up as mezedes are *gigantes* (butter beans cooked in tomato and oil) and *arakas* (peas). *Saganaki*, fried cheese, is another interesting starter. The waiter will raise an eyebrow if mezedes are ordered separately by each individual, even tourists are expected to order a selection and share in Greek style. Salads may be preferred as starters or as part of the starters and the most popular is the village salad or *horiatiki salata* which normally includes lettuce, or cabbage, tomato, onion, cucumber, a certain weight of feta cheese and olives. A few years ago, a salad like this constituted a meal in itself and many tourists were perfectly happy to make a lunch from it. Unfortunately, this made the taverna owner less than happy, consequently the price has risen considerably and they are not always the generous portions they were. Tomatoes, cucumber, feta cheese and lettuce are all offered as separate dishes. Ready cooked

White Peony found in the mountains,
Paeonia clusii ssp rhodia

Rock roses, Cistus creticus, *see*
feature box

The horseshoe orchid, Ophrys
ferrum-equinum

The pink butterfly orchid, Orchis
papilionaceae

The red turban buttercup,
Ranunculus asiaticus

Red poppies, Papaver rhoeas

Top left: Tree frog, Hyla arborea
Top right: Agamo stelio, *lizard*

Right: Dragon's arum,
Dracunculus vulgaris

Cyclamen repandum

Convolvulus althaeoides, *a
pretty bind weed*

Right: Campanula hagielia

dishes may include the familiar *moussaka*, a mince dish with aubergines, potato and bechamel sauce, veal in tomato, *stifado* (veal stew with onions) or *giovetsi* (oven cooked lamb served with pasta). Chicken cooked on the spit is popular and inexpensive but favoured amongst the grills is souvlaki, veal or pork on a skewer. Chops, pork, lamb or veal, are ever present on the evening menus as are *keftedes* (spicy meat balls) and *biftekia* (mince burgers). Fish is sometimes on offer but for a selection it is better to find a fish taverna, *psaria taverna*. *Astakos* (lobster) and *barbounia* (red mullet) are usually top of the menu and are expensive as are *garides* (shrimps). Octopus, grilled or cooked in wine is less expensive as is *kalamari* (squid). At the cheap end is the small *marides* (whitebait) which is eaten in its entirety, head and all. This dish is often available as a starter in a fish restaurant. Deserts are very limited, usually fruit, but the popularity of yoghurt and honey amongst the tourists is now recognised. If you have tucked into your meal with obvious enjoyment, the proprietor may produce a plate of fruit, peeled and presented with his compliments.

Some Greeks prefer to drink ouzo with meals and this is served in small bottles and usually taken with water. Others choose retsina, a resinated wine, which is an acquired taste although the local retsina on Rhodes is very good. There is a wide selection of wines made on the island and these are featured on p.52 & p.139

Apart from Rhodian wines, it is possible that the wine list may contain some of the countries acknowledged good wines like Boutari Naoussa and Lac des Roches as well as some medium priced popular ones like Kambas and Rotonda.

FLORA & FAUNA

The rich and colourful parade of wild flowers on Rhodes is almost totally reserved for the spring months of March, April and May. The long, hot, dry summer is too stressful for plant growth, it is more a test of survival. But the plants do survive using a whole variety of adaptations. Trees and shrubs have made use of deep tap roots to get down nearer the water or devices to minimise water lost by transpiration. Strategies to save water include thick bark, narrow, rolled leaves with minimum surface area, a thick, leathery leaf cuticle, a covering of dense hair, often thick and felty, or special glands to release oil onto the outer surfaces. All these strategies can be seen on Rhodes, not just seen but smelt. It is the oily plants which fill the summer air with that heady, herby aromatic aroma.

For the other plants, it is time to retire for a period of resting. With the annuals, this is easy. All they do is ripen and disperse seed and die, confident that the autumn rains will awake and nourish the next generation. Others, the geophytes, retire to a resting bud below ground and await the passing of summer. These are mostly the plants with below ground storage organs, bulbs, rhizomes or tubers, and there are many of these on Rhodes as there are throughout the Mediterranean where a similar climate persists.

The growth season starts in autumn with the first rains, usually late October. In many ways, this corresponds to early spring in Europe. There is an instant flush of flowers, like *Cylamen graecum, Scilla autumnalis, Sternbergia lutea* and a number of *Colchicum* species. All these leap from the earth straight into flower without the formality of growing leaves, they follow sometime later. Mainly, it is time for steady growth and the dry brown landscape is transformed rapidly into a sea of green as the grass and herbs get underway. Now too is the lambing season if the lush new grass is not to be missed, although it is kids that are more likely to be seen on Rhodes. January begins the next season of flowers, anemones and muscari start to add their colour. February adds still more species to the list but the main display is saved for March and April. By May the greenness of the landscapes has lost all its brightness and brown tones steadily assume command. Lowland flowers diminish rapidly and only in a cool, wet season are there many to be seen by the end of the month. Events are later in the mountains where the floral display is extended for a further week or two.

Significant forests still exist on Rhodes, not as they were 3,000 years ago before man's interference, but there are extensive areas of *Pinus brutia* and *Cupressus sempervirens*. Unfortunately, fire is a natural hazard especially with all the aromatic, highly volatile and highly inflammable oils produced by the plants themselves. It takes so little to start a fire in the forest and the greatest care and vigilance is required by all visitors in summer. Rhodes experienced one of its worst fires in recent history back in 1987. Left to its own devices, burnt areas usually respond with new growth very quickly. A lot of the shrubs in particular are quite resistant and will sprout into growth the next season. Seeds which have lain dormant for perhaps years have a new opportunity and for the following few years there is a great abundance of annuals, biennials and bulb forming plants. The trees restart themselves by seed but take many years to reach maturity. Grazing animals are one of the biggest dangers to the regeneration process. If they are allowed to feed freely on the abundance of new growth and the regeneration checked, the whole process takes a different course. Soil erosion becomes a major factor and, with the loss of humus and water holding capacity, subsequent regrowth is severely hampered.

There are two particular plant communities which the visitor is most likely to notice travelling around the island. The *macchie*, the fairly tall shrub community, usually around shoulder height or more, and the *phrygana* made up of dwarf, knee high shrubs often rounded or domed. There is a fair mixture of species in both

21

communities. In the drier areas, the *macchie* is characterised by shrubs or small trees such as the kermes or holly oak, *Quercus coccifera*, the eastern strawberry tree, *Arbutus andrachne*, the strawberry tree, *A. unedo*, *Erica manipulifera* and *Calicotome villosa*. In damp valley bottoms the myrtle, *Myrtus communis*, *Styrax officinalis* may also be present. Generally, the *macchie* allows little to develop beneath so the ground flora is poor or absent. *Phrygana* is particularly well developed on Rhodes and is generally much more interesting. Two shrubs in particular often dominate, these are *Euphorbia acanthothamnos* and *Sarcopoterium spinosum*. Both are domed, spiny and look as though they are made from wire netting. Their open structure sometimes provides a refuge for wild orchids and, where grazing is heavy, it might be the only place they can survive. There are plenty of other species too making up the *phrygana* including the rock roses which are common on the island. The *phrygana* is open enough to allow a ground flora to develop and is often a good place to look for flowers in the spring, especially annuals and wild orchids.

The fields of red poppies, the yellow and white chrysants and the white anthemis daisies all attract attention but there are some flowers which cause the visitor more excitement than others. One of the stars is the lovely white *Paeonia clusii ssp rhodia* which can be found at a number of locations but chiefly on mount Profitis Ilias. There are three species of cyclamen on the island too, *C. graecum*, which flowers in the autumn and the spring flowering *C. persicum* and the much more common *C. repandum*. There is just one fritillary to find *Fritillaria rhodia* which grows at a number of stations around the island and one tulip, *Tulipa saxatilis* but this is hard to find. Less difficult to find, but still not easy, are the two narcissus, *N. serotinus* and *N. tazetta* but the jewels in the crown are the wild orchids which are widespread around the island. These are featured on p.140.

Mediterranean islands are not especially known for their wildlife but Rhodes is better than most. One of the biggest surprises is the presence of deer on the island although the only ones seen were in captivity. They are the symbol of Rhodes and have pride of place at the harbour entrance. Legend relates that they were introduced in antiquity but it is thought they were reintroduced to the island in the Middle Ages by the Knights of St John and subsequently hunted out of existence by the Turks. The Italians reintroduced them early this century and they may now have been hunted out of existence yet again.

Petaloudes, or the Valley of the Butterflies, one of the more remarkable wildlife features on the island is used as a major tourist attraction. This cool, moist valley is home to the Jersey tiger moth, *Euplagia quadripunctaria*, and it is here that they gather by the thousands for their summer rest. Spread around the valley, they remain huddled on the trees until the autumn. More details are given in the feature on p.126. Generally, it is a good island for butterflies and there is a wide selection to be seen in flight throughout the summer, with May, June and July perhaps the best months.

In antiquity the island was infested with snakes, less so now but they are still around in the countryside although most are harmless. The farmers no longer find it necessary to wear knee length leather boots to guard against the one small species of viper as they did only a decade ago. Lizards too are everywhere but the one to watch out for is the Rhodes dragon, *Agama stellio*. It occurs on a number of Greek islands but not in such numbers as on Rhodes. It is very large and its size, adults can reach 30cm, helps to distinguish it as do the roughly diamond-shaped markings down its back. The colour is variable from light brown to grey with males the more colourful. It likes hot, dry places so keep an eye on stone walls and rocks. Drivers might see it charging across the road at great speed with its head held high. The tree frog is not uncommon on the island and they are mostly spotted basking in the sun on a tree branch usually close to water.

Hunters still regard birds as a delicacy so their activities keep down the numbers but there is still a good variety of small birds amongst which the bee-eater is common. Its liquid chrrup call, once recognised, is very distinctive. Telephone wires are a favourite perch and, in the south of the island particularly, they are present in large flocks. Common too are the hooded crow and the jay but from the acropolis at Lindos it is possible to see colonies of lesser kestrels whilst across on the other coast, at Monolithos, the shy blue rock thrushes are around. Also spotted were woodchat shrike and the black-eared wheatear.

HISTORY

The very early disjointed strands of history coalesce into a story with the formation of the three ancient cities, Ialysos, Kamiros and Lindos. Ialysos on the slopes of Mt Filerimos, just west of the northern tip of the island, seems to have been favoured by the early settlers. Archaeological evidence suggests that the Phoenicians had a settlement there and later, around 1500BC, the Minoans had developed a trading post at nearby Trianda. Significant development took place with the arrival of the Mycenaeans from Achaea about a century later. They brought their own culture, including the Greek language, and the custom of building fortified citadels on strategic hilltops, especially where these guarded fertile plains. In this way the three ancient cities were settled and the island became a flourishing Mycenaean centre.

Next came the Dorians around 1100BC. The Dorians were a Greek speaking tribe who swept down from the north into central and southern Greece to overwhelm first the mainland Mycenaeans then later island communities such as on

Rhodes. They divided the island into three sectors under the cities of Lindos, Ialysos and Kamiros. The following centuries, the Dark Age, up to around 800BC, are vague from a lack of knowledge and understanding, not just of Rhodes but throughout the whole region. Changes in the structure of society mark the end of this period. The autocratic rule of the Mycenaean age gave way to City-states. These enjoyed a more liberal regime which bore elements of democracy and under which the individual had greater freedom of self-expression, intellectually, politically and artistically. Written records too started in this period which gave this first reliable insight into early history. The works of Homer were written down by 750BC in which Ialysos, Kamiros, and Lindos are all mentioned.

SEA TRADE

The island's location made it the focal point of a seaways trading network between east and west and north and south. Routes that ran from Sicily to Argolis then via the Cyclades to Rhodes and on to Cyprus and Syria and from the Ionian coast of Asia minor down through Rhodes to Egypt. Rhodes prospered as evidenced by the coins minted on the island as early as the 6th century BC.

These three cities on Rhodes remained politically independent of each but formed a league with other nearby Dorian cities on Kos and in Asia Minor, Halicarnassus and Knidos, known as the Hexapolis, the six cities. This unity balanced the power of the Ionian cities on Asia Minor. Ultimately, the danger came from a different direction, from Persia, and by 490BC it was coming under attack. By 479BC the island had decided to place itself under the jurisdiction of Athens by joining the Delian Confederacy. It didn't last too long for in 411BC, towards the end of the Peloponnesian War, the island switched allegiance to Sparta.

SYNOECISM

In 408BC, after the break with Athens, the three cities decided to join and found a new trading centre on the northern tip of the island where Rhodes town still stands today. This in turn led to the gradual decline of the original cities. The new city was laid out on a grid system of intersecting streets according to the principles attributed to Hippodamus of Miletus although it is doubtful that Hippodamus himself was directly involved. The town's five harbours were the best equipped in the Aegean which ensured it maintained its strong trading position.

The conquests of Alexander the Great brought even greater trading opportunities for Rhodes in Egypt and Syria so they were quick to side with the Macedonians. Alexander, an admirer of the political system on Rhodes, used it as a model when founding the new city of Alexandria in 331BC. The stability of the island was thrown into turmoil following the death of Alexander. Although Alexander's empire remained unified in the short term, the lack of a royal successor resulted in power passing to the generals in the provinces and it was not long before they were warring between themselves. Antigonus, governor of Syria and Anatolia, took the lead in trying to re-establish unity throughout the empire. Rhodes was strong enough to stand alone and it remained independent. When Antigonus asked Rhodes to join it in battle against Egypt, a major trading partner, it rightly refused. In 305BC, Demetrios the Poliorcet (Besieger), son of Antigonus, launched an attack on Rhodes which is recorded now as one of the most glorious battles in its history.

THE SIEGE

Backed by an army of 40,000 men well armed with the most sophisticated siege machines of the age, Demetrios confidently expected to overthrow the Rhodians mustering around 25,000 soldiers including help from both Crete and Egypt. For a whole year Demetrios tried in vain and even his ultimate weapon, the Helipolis, a nine storey assault tower on wheels of oak, failed to breach the walls, although it did cause considerable damage. After mediation from other Greek cities, Antigonus asked Demetrios to conclude a truce with the Rhodians and withdraw. The treaty guaranteed its independence and upheld the honour of its people. Almost by necessity, Demetrios left

behind the dreaded Helipolis and other heavy siege equipment which was sold and the proceeds used to build an offering to the gods. From this the Colossus of Rhodes, the statue of the sun god Helios was built by Chares of Lindos. The Colossus had a relatively short life. It was destroyed by the violent earthquake of 227BC which also destroyed a large part of the city and the shipyards.

THE PRIME OF RHODES

Rhodes, already a rich and influential city, developed further throughout the Hellenistic period becoming a major centre of learning and of the arts. It came to rival other famous intellectual centres like Alexandria and Pergamum and became one of the main schools of sculpture. Some of the products of Rhodian sculpture, including Aphrodite of Rhodes, are to be seen in the museum in Rhodes old town but most are scattered around and appear in museums throughout the western world. It also attracted painters, poets, and historians but its high reputation was earned mainly by its philosophers and orators. Panaetios, son of Nicagoras, was one of the island's most famous philosophers who eventually became head of the stoic school in Athens.

RHODES & THE ROMANS

In the latter part of the Hellenistic period, Rhodes was increasingly drawn to the emerging power in the west, Rome. Rhodes had a good record in managing its political affairs prudently by the simple expedient of keeping its trading interests central and avoiding taking sides. At the end of the third century, as the Romans grew stronger and showed more interference in Greek affairs, Rhodes decided on taking a friendly attitude to the Romans. It gradually accepted Rome's enemies as her own and became involved in war alongside the Romans against Antiochus III of Syria. Here the Rhodian admiral, Eudamos, defeated Hanibal, the great enemy of the Romans and the military advisor to Antiochus in the sea battle of Side (190BC). In the settlement between Antiochus and the Romans which followed, Caria and Lycia were given to Rhodes. Now Rhodes occupied a position of power but it did not last, nor did the gratitude of the Romans. The Lycians agitated constantly for independence and were frequently complaining about Rhodes to the Roman Senate. When the Rhodians showed reluctance to join the Romans in their battle with Perseus (168BC), the Romans retaliated by taking away Caria and Lycia and by declaring Delos in the Cyclades a free port which destroyed Rhodes' trade at a stroke. Cassius inflicted perhaps the final blow to Rhodes when he laid siege to the island in 42BC with devastating effect. This was a reprisal for the island's refusal to join him against his enemies after the death of Julius Caesar. He was relentless in his destruction, killed many of the inhabitants, stripped off many of the treasures and declared he would leave nothing but the sun.

Rhodes like the rest of Greece, slowly withered away into sad decline hastened by the great earthquake of AD155.

MEDIEVAL RHODES

The history in the early centuries AD after the visit of Saint Paul and the island's conversion to Christianity is at best fragmentary. It is known that the Goths plundered the island in 263 just as they had sacked Ephesus in Asia Minor and Heraion on Samos.

When the Romans divided their empire on a language basis, the Latin speaking west was administered from Rome but the Greek speaking east came under Byzantium. Constantine reunited the empire with leadership from Byzantium which was enlarged to become Constantinople. The empire again divided but this time it became, by 395, a permanent division. The western part of the empire eventually collapsed under the constant assaults of the barbarian invaders but the Byzantine empire survived in the east until around the 11th century. It was by no means a settled existence and the Byzantine empire was constantly under threat especially from Persia. Although Rhodes managed to retain its Greek character, the island suffered invasions from time to time, notably by the Persians in the seventh century and later by the Arabs and the Turks. It never managed to rebuild its trade or recover its former prosperity, at least not until the start of the Crusades.

Rhodes became a staging post on the way to the Holy Land and by 1097 Rhodian ships were carrying supplies to the Crusading armies. In 1191 Richard the Lionheart of England and later Philip of France both docked at Rhodes with their fleets. Venice had established trade with the island perhaps before the Crusades grew in importance and accordingly was granted special privileges by the Byzantine Emperor Alexios Comnenos in 1082. The Venetian's domination of the island lasted only until the Emperor's death. In 1204 when Constantinople was sacked by the Franks, the Byzantine empire was again under threat and the Aegean islands were taken over by various Italian states. Rhodes declared itself independent under the leadership of Leon Gavalas, a wealthy landowner and official of Constantinople. Gavalas was unable to defend the island against hostilities from Venice and an alliance in 1234 returned Rhodes to Byzantium and granted commercial privileges to Venice. There was still no settled existence for throughout the 13th century both the Genoese and the Venetians fiercely contested possession of the island. Genoa emerged triumphant when a treaty signed by Emperor Michael Palaeologos gave it trading supremacy. Soon control of the island was to pass to the Knights of St John.

KNIGHTS OF ST JOHN

The order of the Knights of St John, like the Templars and the Teutonic order emerged from the Crusades. Originally the Knights were a religious and charitable order evolving from a hospice dedicated to St John the Baptist founded by Italian merchants in the eleventh century. Their duties related to the care of Christian pilgrims visiting Jerusalem and they were known as Hospitallers. After the first Crusade, the Hospitallers became more actively involved in the wars against the Moslems and emerged with a military order to extend their protective role beyond nursing and care. It evolved into a structured organisation with the knights representing the military wing, the brothers in charge and the nursing care and the clergy for spiritual matters. In 1291, with the eventual failure of the crusades, the Knights lost their headquarters at Ptolemais in northern Palestine and took refuge in Cyprus. A relatively short time later, in 1306 they bought Rhodes, Kos and Leros from the Genoan admiral Vignolo and three years later they were firmly established on Rhodes (See the feature on p.34 & 35).

THE CASTLES

With the need to defend themselves, the Knights indulged in considerable building activity and rebuilt Rhodes town in such a robust style that it stands hardly changed to this present day. The Acropolis at Lindos was converted to a stronghold and other castles were built around the island, notably at Monolithos, Archangelos, Kritinia, Feraklos and Asklipio. Watchtowers were built around the whole coast and kept manned. The chain of defence against the east stretched to other islands and castles were also built on neighbouring islands including Halki, Symi, Tilos, Nisiros, Kos, Kalymnos and Leros.

Under the protection of the Knights, the native Rhodians were generally loyal but had little political power. Their numbers were swelled by immigrant craftsmen mainly from Spain, Italy and France who were skilled in shipbuilding, engineering, architecture and even in banking. With the Jews being expelled from Spain, a large population built up on Rhodes where they settled in the south-east section of the city.

When the fleet sent by Mohammed II the Conqueror besieged the city in 1480, it was successfully defended by the Knights under the Great Magister Pierre d'Aubusson. Later, in 1522, when besieged by an even greater force under Sultan Suleiman II, the Magnificent, the Knights held out for six months before finally capitulating and leaving for Malta. Rhodes remained under Turkish rule until 1912.

TURKISH RULE,

1522-1912

Events of the Turkish rule are not too well recorded but it seems that Rhodes, as a conquered island, was not granted the privileges which Suleiman granted to other islands in the Dodecanese. Instead, a resident governor was installed with a garrison. The Greeks were excluded from the walled city at night and were obliged to develop new settlements outside.

The Turks were content to assume military control and did not involve themselves in trade or commerce to any great extent and left that to the Rhodians. Soon the island was trading freely with Europe and other parts of the empire and prospering reasonably well. Apart from converting Latin churches into mosques, the Turks made no wholesale attempt to convert the Greeks to Islam and the Rhodians were given almost complete cultural autonomy which proved a major factor in preserving the Greek way of life.

During the Greek revolution against the Turks in the early part of the nineteenth century, Rhodes was unable to participate directly although many islanders went to the mainland to fight. Fearing revolution, the Turks imposed a tighter control on the island and its way of life. In 1866, a campaign was launched to force Rhodes and some of the Dodecanese islands into an Ottoman way of life with Turkish as the official language, the Greek judicial system was replaced by Turkish Tribunals and the Turks took over control of the harbours.

The liberation of Rhodes was a long time coming and when it did finally arrive, in 1912, the island exchanged Turkish masters for Italian.

THE ITALIAN RULE, 1912 -1947

The Italians arrived for a provisional occupation as liberators, they claimed, and not conquerors. Further assurances were given that there would be no interference in the Rhodian way of life or traditions. Free from the Turkish occupation and with all these fine assurances, the Italians were welcomed with open arms. Their promises were soon to prove empty.

At a congress of Dodecanese island delegates in June 1912, it was agreed on a vote the Aegean islands would return to Greece but that was not to be. The treaty of Lausanne (October 1912) returned the Dodecanese to Turkey as soon as the Turks evacuated the Lybian provinces of Cyrenaica and Tripolitania. Events took a different turn when Turkey entered the 1914-18 war. The Italians argued that the Treaty of Lausanne lapsed with the renewed hostilities and laid claim to the Dodecanese islands which they occupied including Rhodes. This was formally acknowledged in the Treaty of London (April 1915). In the peace settlements of 1919-23, agreements were reached with the Italians to assign the Dodecanese back to Greece, with the exception of Rhodes.

Under the Italians the Rhodians suffered a period of oppression and tyranny especially with the rise of Mussolini and Fascism. Local government was dissolved and religious rites suppressed. The schools were taken over and Greek teachers replaced by Italians. The official language and the compulsory language of education became Italian. Land sales were enforced and sometimes expropriated for military use or for Italian immigrants and much was done to destabilise the social structure. On the other hand, money was injected into the economy and with skilled administrators the island saw some benefits. New roads were built and lavish public buildings many of which can still be seen today. They also excavated a number of the sites of antiquity and indulged in a good deal of restoration, but not all of it well done.

Italian occupation was exchanged for German occupation during World War II but Rhodes was eventually liberated by the British and in May 1947 was finally granted union with Greece.

To many, medieval Rhodes Town is Rhodes. Admittedly, the old fortress town is the best preserved of its kind in Europe and a magnet which draws an endless stream of visitors but Rhodes Town is more than that, it is a place which offers something for everyone with a diversity of interest beyond the bastions of the old city walls. In the bustle of busy Mandraki Harbour sailing boats come and go whilst the colourful, teeming streets of modern Rhodes are perfect for those who shop until they drop. All this under the glare of the medieval ramparts looking on with silent envy.

Few towns know the date of their birth but **Rhodes** does. Built to form one economic and political centre, it was founded in 408BC and given the name Damos Rodion (city of Rodians). Until uniting to form the new city, Kamiros, Ialysos and Lindos had functioned as separate city states. Despite losing its political influence, Lindos was the only one of the three to retain importance, the others slipping gradually into obscurity as their populations transferred to the new city. Lindos continued as a major religious centre and thriving port, due in no small measure to its having the only natural harbour on the island and strong defences.

The present day site of Rhodes Town on the north east promontory of the island, the ancients 'Pan's end', was chosen chiefly for its abundant water and harbours. A large triangular plain, it was bounded to the west and south by a range of low hills and open to the sea on the north and east. On the east side lay the three main harbours: the military port (Mandraki, much smaller now than it was then), great harbour (Emborio) and Akandia. Chains across the entrances to the first two harbours were an added protection. Two further harbours, to the west and south east, brought the total to five but these have long since silted up. Traces of the solid piers, built to protect the harbours, can still be traced in the present day moles of St. Nicholas and Myloi (windmills). These harbours, along with a securely protected naval yard, made Rhodes the best equipped port in the Aegean.

The new city of Rhodes had a very different architectural framework from the one we know today. During the time of its prime, in the 2nd and 3rd century BC, it is estimated to have had a population of up to 100,000. More than five times the size of the later medieval town. Rhodes Town was developed in the 'Hippodamean' style from a design attributed to the famous Hippodamus of Miletus. Based on a geometric pattern, this was a system of wide streets rising in straight lines from the harbours in the east to the west, and from north to south cutting each other at regular angles. Walls, 13 kilometres (8 miles) overall in length, formed a barrier on the landward side and apparently circled round to enclose the city. This latter information is found in an oration delivered by one Ailios Aristides to encourage the rebuilding of the city after the AD155 earthquake. 'But the first and foremost wonder that the eyes could not be sated with watching was the circle of the walls and their high and beautiful towers, looking straight as candles to those approaching by sea - '. Possibly an even more impressive sight than their medieval successors! There was the inevitable acropolis on St. Stefanos' hill (modern Monte Smith, see p.56) with the new Hellenistic city spreading from there down the hillside in the direction of the harbours. Some inscriptions found in the area of the present day castle, point to this having been the site of an ancient sanctuary of the sun god Helios. A site which could have existed long before the new city was built. The original area of St John's church of the Knights, near the palace, was also known in medieval times as St Johannes Colossensis. It does not then seem too improbable that this was a possible site for the Colossus of Rhodes, the statue of Helios the sun god (see box, p.33).

Little remains of the original city but recent excavations are helping to build up a better picture. Water was distributed to houses through terracotta pipes which have been found in great numbers beneath road surfaces. Of present day interest, lead pipes were little used for reasons of health, an effect which had been recognised in other cities of the time. The course of most of the ancient streets, especially outside the medieval walls, is little changed to this day. A traveller who visited Rhodes in AD1190 commented that most of the ancient buildings still stood.

Rhodes City lost its importance when the Romans, peeved with them for not willingly joining in their battle against Perseus (168BC), took back Caria and Lycia and granted free port status to Delos. This saw the beginning of the decline in Rhodes' influence. Left prey to marauders and the effects of earthquakes, especially the earthquake of AD155, Rhodes slipped into a steady decline. Its fortunes were not to rise again until the 11th century, when it became a supply station for Crusaders on the way to the Holy Land.

Suddenly, Rhodes was back in favour as the importance of its strategic position became apparent to the developing commercial states of Western Europe. It then became a pawn in a wrestling match between Byzantium, the Genoese and Venetians. Forced out of Palestine by the failure of the Crusades, the Knights of St John set their sights on Rhodes as a new home. In 1306, they bought the island although it was to be a further two years before they secured full control.

With the Knights came the great architectural changes still seen today. These took place in two periods; not by design but as the result of the siege of Mohammed the second in 1480 and earthquakes in 1481. Until 1480 redevelopment was very much a local affair and did not attain the grandeur of the later period which was to last only 42 years but prove extremely productive. This was due in no small measure to the supervision of Grand Master d'Aubusson, who drafted in Western expertise to oversee and build the Gothic style structures to a planned design.

Under the Knights, the walls were strengthened to withstand bombardment by increasingly sophisticated weaponry, their outer walls curved to deflect cannonballs.

The Colossus of Rhodes

Tradition relates how Demetrios, after his defeat by the Rhodians in 305BC, requested his siege equipment be sold and the money used to erect a statue to their victory. Chares of Lindos, a pupil of Lysippos, was commissioned to execute this mammoth task. (Lysippos of Sikyon, was a sculptor who had been attached to the court of Alexander the Great. The 'School of Rhodes' for artists was founded under his influence.) His statue of the sun god Helios, begun in 304BC, took twelve years to complete and was crafted 'in situ', each section being cast in huge heaps of earth so that it was built up in stages.

When completed, the Colossus stood approximately 35 metres high. Depictions for tourist consumption arise from a drawing of a statue straddling the harbour by the Belgian Rottier in 1826. This was based on a somewhat fanciful medieval notion as there are no records as to its pose or siting.

Regarded by the ancients as an outstanding technical and artistic achievement, the Colossus was considered one of the seven wonders of the world. Unfortunately, its period of glory was brief. The great earthquake of 227BC caused it to break at the knees and fall.

For nearly 900 years it lay untouched. Helios (Apollo) was apparently displeased with his statue and through his oracle at Delphi forbade its restoration. The Rhodians, afraid of dire consequences should they disobey such a request, obviously complied. Eventually, when Saracens plundered Rhodes in AD653, the bronze was transported across the sea and sold to a merchant from Edessa. It reputedly took 900 camels to transport the metal. The story was perpetuated even longer, with the said Colossus returning as Turkish cannonballs during the siege of AD1522.

The Knights Hospitallers of St John

The Knights stem from the nursing monks of a hospice founded by Italian merchants in the eleventh century. Known as Brother Hospitallers of St John of Jerusalem, their purpose was to tend Christian pilgrims visiting Jerusalem. Their taste for arms was probably fostered when they extended their care to providing an armed escort service. Fired by the desire to wage war on the 'infidel' after the first Crusade, they turned themselves into a military order whilst still retaining their role as carers of the sick. The forces of Saladin and their bitter rivalry with the Templars, also a military order, was to force them out of Jerusalem to seek a new base.

Only a noble of unblemished character and with Catholic parents could enter the Order as a future Knight. Vows of chastity, obedience and poverty were demanded and the noble could not become a fully fledged Knight before the age of 18. The Order consisted of three classes, a maximum of 600 Knights militant recruited from noble lineage, serving brothers as assistants and nurses and chaplains. The Knights tentacles reached far beyond the bounds of Rhodes and their influence stretched to the administration of their numerous estates in Europe and into every court.

Vanquished from Palestine, the Knights' settled for a short time on Cyprus before purchasing Rhodes. It did not take them long to appreciate the island's merits as a permanent base. Over a period of years their fortifications gained a reputation as models of military architecture, especially the city walls. A powerful fleet of war galleys further enhanced that reputation. To ensure protection from the east they built fortresses on outlying islands, annexed to Rhodes, all of whom had at least one swift dispatch vessel. Thus, along with the 30 castles or so they erected or restored on the island, a strong line of communication was established to warn of imminent attack. As the reputation of the 'Knights of Rhodes' grew so did their coffers. Financed by their estates in Europe, their fortunes were given a boost when the Templars were suppressed in 1312 and some of their forfeited wealth and possessions passed to the Knights on Rhodes.

Although nursing care was still part of the Order's duties, this aspect became blurred as their prime objective moved to defending the church against the 'infidel'. The hospital became the Knights' domain at the expense of the poor and sick, on which the Order was founded.

The Order was divided originally into seven 'tongues' (langues), France, Provence, Auvergne, Spain, Italy, Germany and England which later became eight with the subdivision of Spain into Aragon and Castile. The official language was French but Latin was used for manuscripts. Each group lived in an inn under the leadership of a prior (pilier) and had particular responsibilities, for example, France directed all the Order's hospitals and Italy was Grand Admiral in command of the Knights' fleets. The tongues were also responsible for defending a section of the walls, known as 'curtains' (see medieval city plan). A Grand Master was elected by the

Below inset: *First hospital of the Knights*

Knights to preside over the priors who constituted the Chapter of the Order. His tenure was for life and there were a total of 19 grand masters. Not surprisingly, the majority were French as three of the tongues were French speaking. A political manoeuvre by a Spanish grand master was to split the Spanish tongue into Aragon and Castile and so increase the Spanish vote and influence.

When the Knights were finally defeated by the Turks in 1522 they negotiated a safe departure. It took them seven years to find another home, Malta. As the Knights of Malta they succeeded in keeping the Turks out of the western Mediterranean, especially in 1565 when they were under attack for four months before help arrived. The beginning of the end for the Knights came after the Battle of Lepanto in 1571, when the Turks were defeated by a combined force of European powers assisted by the Order. Interest spread beyond the bounds of the Mediterranean, to the New World and Far East, and the Knights were left behind as other powers developed fleets of sailing vessels. By this time the English Order had ceased to exist, being disbanded when Henry VIII broke away from the church of Rome.

Their end came with the annexation of Malta by Napoleon in 1798 and the confiscation of their French assets after the Revolution. Despite such an ignominious end, their traditions live on in Britain in the form of the St John Ambulance Association.

Gates were a weak link in the fortification. Of the original eight, some were blocked off or re-sited and a complicated double moat and drawbridge system constructed which can still be seen at the Amboise and Koskinou gates. The inner moat was purposefully left dry to deter the building of siege towers. Forts were constructed at the end of the harbour moles to increase protection. St Nicholas Fort guarding the naval harbour of Mandraki still stands. Little remains of the square Naillac Tower, destroyed last century, which along with the French Tower stood at the entrance to the Commercial Harbour (Emborio) with a heavy chain slung between. Fifteen windmills stood along the mole of the French Tower which retains the name of Mole of the Windmills, not to be confused with the three Mandraki windmills. Crowning these impressive fortifications was the Palace of the Grand Masters, a fortress within a fortress, built on the site of an ancient temple to Helios (later Apollo).

Compared with the size of the Hellenistic city, the medieval fortress city was much smaller. A low inner wall separated the Knights' quarters or Collachium (Kastellos), which housed all the buildings associated with their order, from the rest of the town (Bourg) where the merchants lived. The Knights barely had time to enjoy their new quarters before the ever present Moslem threat erupted. Under Suleiman the Magnificent, the Turks mounted a siege on the island which lasted for 177 days before the Knights finally capitulated.

Despite a stay of 390 years, the Turks contributed little by way of new building. In fact, they inadvertently caused the destruction of prime medieval treasures in a spectacular explosion, which left many hundreds of people dead. A long forgotten cache of gunpowder, stored somewhere beneath the Palace of the Grand Masters and Church of St John when Suleiman the Magnificent captured Rhodes, exploded after lightning struck in the vicinity of the Church and started a fire. The Church of St John was razed, the Inn of Germany completely disappeared and all that was left of the Palace of the Grand Masters was a burnt out shell.

Gradually, the medieval city began to take on an oriental look. Turkish elements, such as wooden balconies and window lattices, were added to the existing buildings and, with the addition of a minaret, churches were converted into mosques. The Turks did build some imposing mosques, including those of Suleiman and Retzep Pasha. They also built several *hammams* (public baths) but the only one in use now is the Mustafa Pasha hammam. Eastern type houses also appeared. These either opened onto the street or were entered through gardens or courtyards.

When the Turks arrived, they took over the Collachium and a large part of the Bourg allocating the eastern end to the Jews and expelling the Greeks. The Greeks could enter the city by day but had to leave, on pain of death, at night. As a result of this, new settlements developed outside the city walls along the remains of the ancient road network. The Greeks built six quarters, or '*Marasia*', outside the city walls which still exist today; St Anastasia, St Anargyrous, St Nicholas, St George, Masari and Neochori. Fortunately, the 4km of city walls remained virtually untouched and this preservation was due in no small measure to the Turks using land immediately outside the walls as cemeteries.

After the Turks came the Italians in 1912. They were responsible for the reconstruction of the Palace of the Grand Masters, destroyed by the gunpowder explosion of 1856, and the Italian buildings fronting Mandraki Harbour. Whilst in control, the Italians were prolific builders, restorers and excavators of ancient sites. Many of the Turkish embellishments, especially those tacked onto Medieval buildings, were dismantled under their rule. Churches that had been changed into mosques were reconsecrated and the skyline robbed of many of its minarets. Much of the Italian legacy remains intact within Rhodes Town. The Italians were to be ousted themselves in 1943 when German forces occupied the island.

Modern day Rhodes Town has burgeoned under the mantle of tourism. The Greeks' love affair with concrete has manifested itself in the usual erosion of space without yielding anything of architectural merit. No lessons seem to have been learnt even from the relatively recent Italian era.

Fortunately, the medieval walls and Italianate buildings along Mandraki conceal this modern metropolis of narrow streets and clustered concrete buildings. In spite of its shortcomings, including the less than friendly 'take it or leave it' attitude now prevalent in high density tourist centres, Rhodes Town has much to offer the visitor. A medieval atmosphere, with a modern flavour, is more likely to be conjured up in the old city by those willing to stir themselves early or linger late into the evening under the stars.

Rhodes Town lies at the northern tip of the island. A finger of heavily developed land pointing along the imaginary line which divides the Aegean and Mediterranean seas. In this area are to be found most of the newer hotels. For a quieter more authentic ambience, it is worth seeking out the smaller, less sophisticated hotels tucked into the maze of streets in the old town. Besides hotels there is a plethora of pensions and rooms available yet, despite a seeming abundance of accommodation, Rhodes' popularity with tour operators and an invasion of visitors during high season creates a scarcity. If a gourmet experience is essential to your stay then again, Rhodes can offer just about anything to satisfy most palates. Spring is a good time to visit but, come before 1st April and the tourist streets in the old city will still be closed and shuttered.

There is no substitute for exploring on foot. The four tours outlined below cover both the new and old towns. Apart from its harbour front and Turkish cemetery, the main draw of the new town is its upmarket shopping. The old town bursts into life in summer and becomes the hub around which everything else revolves. Its maze of narrow streets, archways and courtyards invite exploration and promise a new discovery around every corner. Winter exposes a very different face when even the locals complain about the lack of things to do but, for those who wish to avoid the trappings of tourism, it is good time to come and wander at leisure.

A surprising plus point is the availability of clean and free WCs, also to be found in the museums. Traffic is banned from the old town, except to residents, whilst in the new, parking and one-way streets are a confusion in themselves. The best option for those with a car, staying outside the town, is to park in the suburbs and walk in. When entering a church or mosque, the

usual rules of dress apply i.e. no skimpy clothing, which includes shorts and sleeveless tops usually. In addition, should a mosque be entered, visitors are required to remove their footwear at the entrance. This is a practical ruling, to protect the carpets covering the floor on which the men sit for prayer.

TOUR 1.

MEDIEVAL HIGHLIGHTS

Prepare for an assault on the senses on entering the old town. The stoic grandeur of the medieval fortress-like buildings seem at odds with the narrow alleyways and homespun architecture of the houses. Graceful minarets, rickety balconies, tranquil squares with fountains and shady trees still exude an oriental air. Turkish influences are all around with blue glass eyes to ward off evil, Turkish delight simply renamed *loukouma* on sale and restaurants offering a cuisine which owes as much to the Turks as it does to the Greeks.

A visit to all or some museums is usually on everyone's list and there is a money-saving ticket available which gives entry to four of the main museums in the old town. Even if ancient remains do not excite, the **Museum of Decorative Arts** with its insight into life during the past couple of hundred years, will interest all the family. If time is pressing, and there is only time for one museum visit, save it for the Palace of

Opposite inset: The Turkish cemetery near the casino *Above:* Old town walls
Below left: Ipoton street leading up to the Palace of the Grand Masters
Below right: Palace of the Grand Masters

the Grand Masters. The Exhibition of Archaeological Excavations, displaying finds from Prehistoric to Hellenistic times is clear, informative and above all fascinating. The Palace closes at 3pm and admittance to the museum stops at 2.30pm but the exhibition demands much longer than half an hour.

From the taxi stand in Platea Rimini, head past the ranks of sponge sellers and portrait painters to enter the old town through the Freedom Gate (Pili Eleftherias). This narrow bridge has to cope with a steady stream of traffic, in both directions, as well as a swell of tourists.

Once inside, leaving the traffic to hurtle left out through the Arsenal Gate, head up the right-hand side of Platea Simis. The tour starts in the **Collachium**, the Knights' preserve. To the left are the remains of a 3rd century BC Temple of Aphrodite and in front of this is a useful map showing the layout of the town. Opposite here is the **Ministry of Culture Museum Shop**. For a piece of Greek history to take home, look no further. On sale are authentic casts of parts of friezes and funeral stele and replicas of ancient Greek jewellery.

Further up the rise, on the left, facing partially onto Platea Argirokastrou, is the **Inn of Auvergne** built in 1507 and more recently restored. A Byzantine baptismal font serves as an unusual fountain in the Argirokastrou square and heaps of cannonballs, from the Turkish siege of 1522, are displayed as decoration. One of the earliest buildings in the Collachium

fronts the square, the colour and texture of its stonework softened by a tumbling mass of bougainvillaea. This was originally the **Palace of the Armeria**, constructed under the Grand Master Roger de Pinsot in the 14th century, and the First Hospital of the Knights. It was also used by the Knights and Turks as an arsenal but today it enjoys a more peaceful role, it houses the offices of the **Archaeological Institute of the Dodecanese** and is where the first museum is located.

The Museum of Decorative Arts: an off-putting title for a delightful and intimate Folk Art Museum where decorated tiles, intricately carved woodwork, brightly coloured Rhodian style pottery and exquisite needlework are elegant reminders of an earlier culture. A reconstruction of the interior of a traditional Rhodian house provides a good insight into everyday life. Even here, a Turkish influence can be detected. Many exhibits seem to originate from the Island of Symi where women could appear well provided with rich dresses by owning just one long, sleeveless, elaborately embroidered 'gilet' to wear over a basic plain dress embroidered only round the neck, hem and sleeves.

On the opposite side of the road is the 13th century **Byzantine Church of St Mary**, (Panagia tou Kastrou or Virgin of the Fort), which became the first cathedral of the Knights. A forced change of allegiance under Turkish rule saw its steeple converted into a minaret and renamed Enderoum. After a Christian massacre here in 1523 it became known to Rhodians as the 'red mosque'. Converted back again for use as a Christian church it has become a fitting home for the **Byzantine Museum**.

Byzantine Museum: contains an exhibition of well displayed Byzantine paintings and frescos in an atmospheric setting. One fresco has even been transferred from Halki and is displayed on the ceiling of the barrel vault.

The cobbled street Odos Ipoton, the Street of the Knights, rises up right to the Palace of the Grand Masters. For the moment though, continue into Platea Moussieo (Museum). Tucked back on the left is a bank, separated from the rather undistinguished **Inn of England** by a narrow street. A plaque on the wall of the Inn here is the only indication that the building is of any significance. Rebuilt to the original plan a century after its destruction in 1856, the Second World War again left it in need of repair. Of more interest are the eateries along the narrow alley which leads off the far left-hand corner of the square beyond the Inn.

The impressive building to the right commands attention. This was the new **Hospital of the Knights** and their original 'raison d'être'. Begun in 1440, over the remains of a Roman building, it wasn't until the Grand Master d'Aubusson took charge over 40 years on that it was completed. It was built along similar lines to Byzantine hostelries. Eight plain arches support the facade, the only relief to the severe exterior being the decorative, recessed Gothic arch of the main gateway which lies

beneath the projection of the chapel above. Unfortunately, the original wooden main gate found its way to Versailles when it was sold by the Turks last century. After the Knights' departure it was used variously as a hospital then ignobly as a barracks. Skilfully restored by the Italians and again after suffering bomb damage during the Second World War it now serves as the **Archaeological Museum**.

Archaeological Museum: the entrance opens into a courtyard, surrounded by a galleried upper storey accessed by an outside stairway. Stone fragments and stacks of cannonballs, relics from various sieges, lie on the ground and a first century BC marble statue of a crouching lion takes centre spot. Upstairs is the large room which was the Infirmary Ward. What the small windowless rooms down the sides were used for is open to conjecture, possibly isolation wards or maybe wardrobes. Pilgrims came here for treatment until the needs of the Knights themselves became paramount. When this happened, the vow of poverty seems to have been conveniently forgotten! Simple wooden beds were replaced by beds decked with brocaded canopies and nothing less than silver plate was good enough to eat off. Some imagination is needed to conjure up what this bare room must have looked like fully furnished.

Medieval gives way to an earlier era in other rooms along the gallery. It is difficult not to admire the art of the sculptor in Hellenistic times and the marble statuette of

Aphrodite bathing, an adaptation of an earlier first century BC sculpture, is a fine example. There is also another sculpted Aphrodite from the third century BC more commonly known as the Marine Venus after being hauled out of the sea nearly seventy years ago. It is this sculpture which inspired the title of Lawrence Durrell's book 'Reflections on a Marine Venus' about his life on Rhodes. A second century BC head, from a statue of the Sun God Helios driving his chariot in the sky, still has the holes where iron spikes for the sun's rays would have been positioned. It is thought that this was sited in the Temple to Helios. Grave stele, as here, provide an insight into the everyday life of ordinary people of the time. One from Kamiros depicts a fifth century BC bas-relief of a girl saying good-bye to a dead mother and another, erected by Damokles to his dead wife Kalliaista, shows her seated in front

of her maid. Besides these gems there are many funerary objects which is not too surprising, as most of the information gleaned about this early period comes from ancient cemeteries. Pottery figures strongly, especially Geometric and there are also some mosaics.

Leaving the Collachium with its austere façades, it is time for a complete change of scene. What greater contrast can there be than the Turkish bazaar atmosphere of **Sokratous Street!** From hereon, souvenir shops jostle for attention with displays of gold and silver, leather, lace and the inevitable T-shirts.

Continuing in the same direction, outdoor tables on the square at Polydorou are invitingly placed for the thirsty visitor and it is tempting to pause and watch the world go by. Moving on through the square, Sokratous is not difficult to miss. Its wide bustling street, reminiscent of its central role in the old bazaar rises up towards the **Mosque of Suleiman**, With the projecting wooden balconies (sachnisi) of its Turkish style buildings, this is the most famous and photographed street in the old town. A short diversion left here leads into Platea Ipokratous, beyond which is the medieval courthouse and stock exchange, the **Kaste-llania**, and close by the impressive **Marine Gate**.

Wandering up Sokratous could take a long time. Colour spills onto the street as traders entice with their assortment of wares, ikons, replica helmets, embroidery,

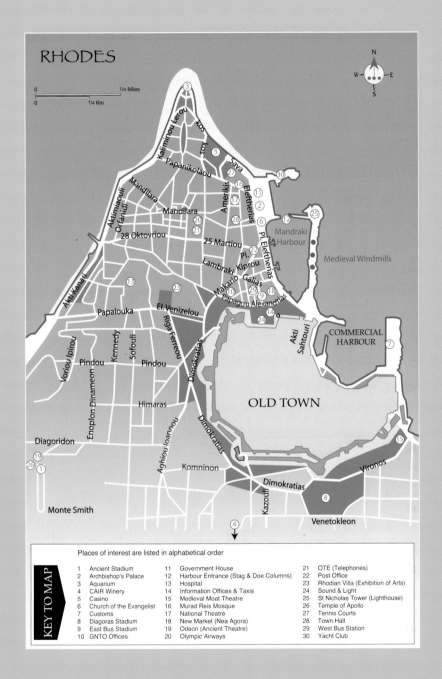

RHODES

0 ____ 1/4 Miles
0 ____ 1/4 Km

Kaliminou Lerou
Papanikolaou
Mandilara
Mandilara
Aktimiaouli
Orfanidi
28 Oktovriou
kos
kos
Sava
Amerikis
Eleftherias
Pl. Eleftherias
25 Martiou
Pl.
Lambraki
Kiprou
Makario
Galias
Papagou Alexandrias
Akti Kanari
El. Venizelou
Papalouka
Riga Fereou
Voriou Ipirou
Kennedy
Sofouli
Pindou
Pindou
Enoplon Dinameon
Himaras
Dimokratias
Diagoridon
Aghiou Ioannou
Dimokratias
Komninon
Monte Smith
Kazouli
Dimokratias
Venetokleon
Vironos

Mandraki Harbour
Medieval Windmills
COMMERCIAL HARBOUR
OLD TOWN
Akti Sahtouri

Places of interest are listed in alphabetical order

KEY TO MAP			
1	Ancient Stadium	11	Government House
2	Archbishop's Palace	12	Harbour Entrance (Stag & Doe Columns)
3	Aquarium	13	Hospital
4	CAIR Winery	14	Information Offices & Taxis
5	Casino	15	Medieval Moat Theatre
6	Church of the Evangelist	16	Murad Reis Mosque
7	Customs	17	National Theatre
8	Diagoras Stadium	18	New Market (Nea Agora)
9	East Bus Stadium	19	Odeon (Ancient Theatre)
10	GNTO Offices	20	Olympic Airways
21	OTE (Telephones)		
22	Post Office		
23	Rhodian Villa (Exhibition of Arts)		
24	Sound & Light		
25	St Nicholas Tower (Lighthouse)		
26	Temple of Apollo		
27	Tennis Courts		
28	Town Hall		
29	West Bus Station		
30	Yacht Club		

Opposite: The famous Socrates street lacking its minaret, removed after earthquake damage in 1991. Rhodes old town carpet weaving, ceramics and leather sandals all clamouring for attention. Pastry shops and cafés seduce the foot weary whilst the lure of shady alleyways suggest more peaceful oases. An arch jutting out into the street, the Aga Mosque, has so far restricted the view ahead but from hereon the Mosque of Suleiman comes into better focus. Minus its minaret it no longer dominates the skyline on this approach as seismic activity in 1991 so weakened its structure it had to be dismantled for the sake of safety. Its restoration has been in hand for the last decade but some work has started on the mosque itself. The loss of the minaret has certainly diminished the character of this otherwise fascinating street.

The Mosque of Suleiman was built on the site of an earlier Church of the Apostles and erected in honour of the Sultan after his conquest of Rhodes in 1522. It was rebuilt in 1808. For the moment one can only peer through the locked gates at its rotting wood and crumbling pink cement to imagine its former magnificence but it is under renovation. The pink colour on many old buildings is not paint but a special pink cement used for waterproofing on floors, roofs, domes and walls.

Do not continue up past the mosque but go right in front of it along Panetiou. The commanding walls of the **Palace of the Grand Masters** loom ahead. On the left are excavations of medieval buildings behind which is the Turkish school constructed on the site of the Conventual Church of St John destroyed in the 1856 gunpowder explosion, a fragment of wall being the sole remains. Built in a plain architectural style during the 14th century it contained the tombs of the Knights; remnants of which are found in the Knights Hospital. Pass the top of the 'Street of the Knights' to enter the Palace environs. At the end of the street is Platea Kleovoulou and the restored loggia which, when the Knights were in residence on the island, connected the Palace with the Church of St John. Two round towers announce the entrance to the Palace, its large pointed door being one of the parts preserved from the original building.

The Palace of the Grand Masters: standing on the highest part of the Collachium, the Palace was built on the probable site of the Sanctuary of Helios in the 14th century. (Helios was the original sun god on Rhodes but he appears to have been supplanted at some later time by Apollo who was also a sun god as well as sometime god of light, poetry, music etc. The role of gods were manipulated by different peoples to suit their personal requirements.) Designed as a fortress in its own right with underground storerooms to withstand siege, it served as the Grand Masters' residence and the hub of the Knights' activities. Although it survived the Turkish siege of 1522 little damaged, its use as a prison and the earthquake of 1851 hastened structural decline. The gunpowder explosion and fire five years later, coupled with removal of stone for other building work by the Turks, effectively sealed the fate of this once commanding edifice.

Left to languish for the next 80 years, it took a new master to restore its fortunes when, under the Italians in the 1930s, it was rebuilt as an intended summer residence for Victor Emmanuel III and Mussolini. The exterior is supposed to follow the style of the old building with the interior adapted more to modern day requirements with electricity and central heating. Even camouflaged lifts were installed so as not to appear incongruous in such a setting. Ostentation was more a prerequisite than taste when it came to interior design, or so it seems. The lavish style extends to the use of Roman and Byzantine columns and importation of some fine Roman and Early Christian mosaics from Kos.

The entrance to the main body of the Palace is up the sweep of stairs to the left, opposite the pay desk immediately on entering. Inscriptions near this entrance appertain to the Italian Fascist regime and to Greek Independence gained in 1947. Ahead is the inner courtyard with its display of Roman statuary. The exhibition covers the period from Prehistoric times to the Hellenistic City and includes some excellent mosaics. It is well annotated and displayed and time spent absorbing the information in here really helps to recreate the living and breathing Rhodes of old. Climb the stairs to wander through the corridors and spacious rooms open to the public where a combination of seemingly wall to wall mosaics, statues, Italian Renaissance carving and scant furnishings add to the sterile atmosphere. This mix of periods lie uneasily together. Views from the windows over the town and gardens give a different perspective as does a walk along the old city walls.

Walking the walls is an excellent way to appreciate them as a tremendous feat of fortification. It also provides a superb overview of the old town which helps to put the layout into perspective. Only accessible on Tuesdays and Saturdays at 2.30pm. Tickets at the entrance to the Palace. This unguided walk starts up the steps and through the small Cannon Gate off the outer courtyard. Covering only about a third of its original length, the walk passes along the 'Curtains' defended by Auvergne, Aragon and England, in that order, ending at the Koskinou Gate. Descend into Efthimiou and follow right then round left along Dimosthenous to Platea Evreon Martiron, the **Square of the Jewish Martyrs** which is easily identified by its tasteless modern fountain of bronze seahorses. The square was renamed in memory of the remaining Jewish population, who were deported from this spot to concentration camps when the Germans arrived in 1943. Only a few Jewish families live in the old town now out of a population numbering 6,000 before 1939, a fortunate 4,000 of whom emigrated at the outset of war. Close by, in Dosiadou, can be located the synagogue. The next street out of the square on the left leads to the **Ibrahim Pasha Mosque**

Mustafa Pasha Turkish Baths or Hammam

The original baths were built in 1558, during the early days of the Turkish occupation, and updated 200 years later when Mustafa Pasha built the mosque next door. This upgrade raised them to such a level of sophistication that they attracted visitors from the Ottoman mainland. Not only were they used for cleansing, they were also great meeting places as, centuries before, the Roman baths had been. To some extent they still function in much the same way today except that the main users are Greek with the Turks and tourists making up the minority. Worth a visit if only for a peep into a world little changed by the passage of time.

Men and women attend on alternate days. Decorative and plain marble is used to full effect inside and a good level of cleanliness maintained. The coolness of the changing cubicles contrasts sharply with the humidity level on the far side of a weighted door. Plunged into a maze of cubicles with bath or shower it is easy to become disorientated. The grand central room, with its domed ceiling, takes on an ethereal quality when its marble opulence is viewed through a steamy mist. Here, cold tap water is provided in individual carved marble water troughs. Amazingly, the water is still heated by the original log fire system, whose insatiable appetite must have consumed acres of olive trees down the centuries, and distributed along a network of pipes under the floor. A visit here is an experience in itself and stimulates a feeling of *joie de vivre* - try it!

and very pleasant Platanos Square, reputed to have been used as a place of execution by the Turks with the **Demerli Mosque** lying a little further along. This is also a good area for exploring the numerous alleyways with less touristy shops. Sokratous lies just north of here.

Leaving the Palace, go left down Ipoton, the '**Street of the Knights**', one of the best preserved medieval streets in existence. Besides being the main route from the Palace to the port through the Collachium, it is the location of the Inns of the various Tongues. The present day pristine appearance of the cobbled street is thanks in no small measure to the Italians, who dismantled the Turkish addition of rickety wooden balconies to restore the late medieval architecture. Restoration alone though does not bring buildings to life. Now used mainly as offices, it lacks the buzz of habitation and shows itself for what it has become – a museum piece, nevertheless, it is an impressive street. Even before it gained its medieval mantle it was an ancient route to the port. From this angle, the first point to catch the eye is an arch spanning the street. The

Inn of the Tongue of Spain lies to the right either side of the arch and the room above the arch belongs to it whilst opposite is the later built, more elaborate, **Inn of the Tongue of Provence**.

Lower down on the left is the small fourteenth-century church of Agia Triada (Holy Trinity) attached to the **Inn of France** which was converted by the Turks to a mosque called Han-Zade and before the chapel the house belonging to its chaplain. Well down the street now, reach the richly ornamented **Inn of the Tongue of France** on the left where the coats of arms of France, with its three lilies and royal crown, and the Grand Master d'Aubusson with its cardinal's hat can be seen in a carved frame, dated 1495. The building across the road, next to the hospital, had connections with the Inn of Spain. Finally, near the bottom of the street on the left, is the **Inn of the**

Tourist trains

Motorised trains have made an appearance in many of the bigger resorts on the island. They convey tourists between popular places of interest and run to a regular timetable. Not only do they run in Rhodes town but also in Faliraki, Archangelos and Afandou. It seems certain they will appear in other places before long.

In Rhodes town the train starts outside the National Theatre, just north of Mandraki Harbour, and is particularly useful for reaching Monte Smith. It does not enter the old town but tours just outside the walls before climbing up to Monte Smith. The train runs hourly, details at the end of this chapter, and there is a small charge.

The tourist train reaching Monte Smith

Shopper's guide

Rhodes is a Mecca for bargain hunters and lives up to its reputation as a shopper's paradise. Most items are cheaper here than anywhere else in Greece due to special tax concessions conferred on the island when it was united with Greece in 1947. Spirits are definitely a good buy, with prices in the shops lower than the duty free shop at the airport and it pays to buy now rather than at departure. Choose from ready-to-wear designer labelled clothes or have them tailor-made within a matter of days from bargain fabrics, which include genuine Harris tweed and cashmere, and also leather and silk. Leather shoes are a good buy and the traditional soft leather boots can be made to measure. Handmade jewellery is a speciality in silver or 18-carat gold which is usually sold by weight, the price depending on current market rates. Umbrellas are everywhere and it is possible to buy one for every conceivable occasion. Sponges feature strongly in tourist areas (see Symi Chapter 9) and other good buys are herbs, spices and local honey. Add to all this a bewildering array of local handicrafts, pottery, olive wood carving, metal craft, embroidery and weaving and there is enough to keep the most ardent shopper occupied for many a day.

Bargaining is possible, especially in the souk-like atmosphere of the old town, and price reductions possible in jewellers but usually only on a cash payment basis.

Authentic souvenirs

Tongue of Italy with its exterior showing simpler lines than those of the Inn of France.

TOUR 2.

THE OLD QUARTER

A voyage of discovery lies awaiting intrepid explorers willing to explore the maze of alleyways and streets of the old town. Medieval and Turkish styles blend to create a unique and intriguing atmosphere within the confines of the old walled town. Tucked away in here are countless small workshops where skilled craftsmen still practise their art in much the same way as their ancestors. Although this tour follows a defined route, it is only a guideline and forays where the fancy leads add to the enjoyment. Keeping a map to hand can help, even if only to make sure not too many ever decreasing circles are tramped although a number of principal streets assist in making some order out of seeming chaos. Sokratous leads down from the Mosque of Suleiman towards the harbour, continuing as Aristotelous then Pindarou as it skirts round parallel with the Commercial Harbour. A rough grid of streets south of Sokratous is formed by Ipodamou, Fanouriou, Pythagora and Omirou. Many of the small hotels and pensions are to be found in the tortuous network of narrow lanes within this grid. The Bourg shows an equally fascinating face by night when murmuring voices, clinking glasses, bouzouki music, soft shadows and twinkling lights change leafy plateas into magical enclaves. This walk could take all day if a lunch in ambient surroundings, haggling over souvenirs and frequent pit stops for a drink is part of the equation.

Enter the old town via the d'Amboise Gate off Dimokratias. There is no mistaking the narrow entrance road lined with lace and souvenir stalls. With a swirl of activity going on all around, the magnificence of the gate itself is easily overlooked. Entry through this early 16th-century gate, one of the most impressive of all the gates, allows for an appreciation of the complicated defensive structure of the fortifications. Through the gate, a gauntlet of artists all too willing to draw your portrait attract an audience along the shaded walled road of the inner fortifications. Sensibly, the portrait painters here along with those on the approach to the port entrance, Freedom Gate, have formed a union. Instead of fighting for the best position, they agree to rotate on a regular basis.

Once out of the confines of the walls, the rich tapestry begins to unfold. Restaurants and souvenir shops compete for attention but stopping along here for a drink might surprise the unwary. The result of a casual beer order could be an outsize trumpet-shaped glass of German beer, containing enough liquid to slake the thirst of a few. By now, the clock tower 'To Roloi' will probably have captured attention. This offers the highest viewpoint in town. It was built in 1852 on the site of a previous tower and formed a corner of the wall which ran parallel with the Street of the Knights to the port, separating the Collachium from the Bourg. It is open every day and the entrance price includes a soft drink or coffee.

Head across the top of Sokratous past the Mosque of Suleiman (Tour 1) and, on the right, is the **Turkish Library of Ahmet Havuz**, whose collection includes a chronicle of the siege of 1522 and two illuminated Korans of the 15th and 16th centuries. Immediately after the library, keep right to enter **Ipodamou**. Immediately, the narrow cobbled street transports the visitor into a different age blanking out the hustle and bustle of the main tourist thoroughfare. Arches, protection against earthquakes, bridge the street, enticing alleyways, flower decked courtyards all exude a more tranquil air. Even the tourist shops become less intrusive. Divert left along Arhelaou, by the

Symposium Garden Restaurant, to Platea Arionos and the Turkish Baths. Dominated by the **Mustafa Pasha Mosque and Baths** of the same name, the square provides another opportunity to sit at one of the cafes and absorb the atmosphere. This Turkish Bath (hammam) still functions, despite bomb damage during World War II, and subsequent renovation work is difficult to detect to the non expert (see box p.46).

For some excellent Greek dancing, an evening visit to the **Nelly Dimoglou Theatre** on Andronikou, behind the baths, is a must. Performances take place Monday, Wednesday and Friday at 9.20pm from May to October but the gardens are open every day. Return to Ipodamou to continue down the street. On approaching the walls ahead turn left, opposite number 46. (This route does not go past the St Nicholas Hotel on the left, just after this turn off point, but it looks an inviting place to stay.) An intriguing wend through a narrow alleyway leads onto Omirou, emerging by the Ancient Market Garden Bar. Continue left along the street. There are better opportunities for sideways exploration and capturing a real flavour of the old town in this area.

Pass the end of Fanouriou, by Hotel Paris, to shortly turn left through an archway into Platea Dorieos with its domed fountain which makes a great setting for eating out under the trees. Tucked into a corner, and almost masked by a taverna, is the old Byzantine church of Agios Fanourios but dominating the square is the **Retzep Pasha Mosque**. It was one of the first buildings erected after the Ottoman conquest in 1522 and one of the most striking. It is currently under renovation so the public may soon be able to view the interior, said to be a unique example of Islamic architecture.

To regain Fanouriou, cross the square to the left, from the entry point, then turn right. Fanouriou is one of the oldest streets in the old town and can be better appreciated at this lower end. As the street rises up towards the Collachium, an increase in souvenir shops announces the return to the tourist heart. Emerge onto Sokratous by the Aga Mosque.

TOUR 3. MANDRAKI & SHOPPING

Most of the new town has developed since the Italian occupation of 1912. The added impetus of tourism, especially during the past 20 years, has greatly accelerated development even further. Besides being the shopping, administrative and business quarter, the northern tip also contains most of the hotels and revolves around the tourist industry. **Mandraki Harbour** is part of this quarter and a buzzing meeting place for locals and tourists alike. To the west, especially on the slopes of Monte Smith, are to be found leafy suburbs with larger houses and villas whilst the south has the densest population and the south east most of the light industry.

Although this tour concentrates on the northern section, a walk round the outside of the old town walls is not without interest, nor a walk or drive down the Lindos road to Rodini Park where the famous Rhodes 'School of Rhetoric' was located. The wooded park was designed and laid out by the Italians who populated it with deer and peacocks. According to legend, the Delphic oracle urged the intro-duction of deer as a means of ridding the island of snakes but, when the Italians arrived, all signs of deer had disappeared. Unfort-unately, as with much of the Italian legacy, neglect has taken its toll and the deer have been long gone from the park. Also in the vicinity is a large Hellenistic rock tomb, wrongly named 'tomb of the Ptolemies'.

Breakfast in the New Market (Nea Agora) makes a fitting start to this tour, as most local activity starts early. Using Rimini Square as the starting point, and before heading for Mandraki, wander into the lush gardens beneath the castle walls where the 'son et lumiére' is held. The flowers here create a riot of colour, softening the gaunt crenellated walls of the Palace towering above. It is never too early for coffee, so it is straight to the harbour front and the New Market. An irregular seven sided construction built by the Italians in the Turkish style, this building displays an unusual departure from the more severe lines of their other building work. Round the outside are crowded numerous snack bars,

Opposite inset: Church of the Evangelist, Mandraki Harbour

The C.A.I.R (K.A.I.R) Winery

The Company Agricultural Industry of Rhodes was started by the Italians in 1928, although the island recently celebrated 2,400 years of wine making. Now Greek owned and operated, the company produced a special white wine, Rodos 2400, to celebrate that milestone in history. A story from those early days tells how the Cretans, jealous of Rhodes' fame for high quality wine, copied Rhodian amphorae in an attempt to pass off their own wine as Rhodian.

The grapes preferred by CAIR are grown in vineyards on the western side of the island, particularly around Embonas. Here many small vineyards are located in specific cooler microclimates where granite stones in the soil help by increasing humidity which in turn improves the flavour. Athiri, a very old local variety of white grape, is grown in vineyards on lower slopes below Embonas whilst mountain regions produce a better quality of red grape. Vineyards are specially selected for the quality of grapes used under each specific label and are constantly monitored.

The original site for wine production in Rhodes Town has all but closed down and production is now concentrated at the new plant, just outside Rhodes town on the Lindos road, where the latest technology is employed.

CAIR labels include:-

Ilios: Dry white from the Athiri grape.

Chevalier de Rhodes: Dry red from the Mandilaria. Said to be the same wine drunk by the 'Knights'. An acceptable red wine frequently on offer in tavernas.

Platoni: A semi-sweet white, rosé or red table wine from the Athiri and Mandilaria grapes.

Moulin: A white, rosé, red, dry and semi-dry table wine. Produced from a mix of varieties including Cabernet Sauvignon and Grenache. The semi-dry white and rosé, with a light, delicate flavour are particularly palatable with a meal or on their own.

Rodos 2400: A dry white from the Athiri grape.

Arxontiko. (Chateau): A dry red wine from a mix of grapes. Lovers of red wines will appreciate the subtle hint of blackcurrant – best of the reds!

Muscat de Rhodes: A sweet white wine of the Moschato variety.

Amandia: A sweet red wine.

Retsina: Natural resin and the Athiri grape combine to make this an excellent lightly resinated crisp white wine.

CAIR Brut & Demi-Sec: A very drinkable sparkling wine from the Athiri grape.

Nisiotikos: Available in large as well as standard size bottles, this white, rosé or red wine is ideal for general use.

cafés and all manner of small shops selling herbs, spices, nuts, olives and duty free wines and spirits. Rhodes is a duty free island and spirits are cheap. Inside the huge and colourful tree shaded courtyard, fresh fruit and vegetable stalls, butchers, tourist paraphernalia and cafés combine in a kaleidoscope of constant activity. The large centrepiece has a dual function, fish market above and underneath, free WC's. Most of the fish market activity seems to take place around eight in the morning, with the fresh catch spilling out into the courtyard area. *Tiropitta*, *souvlakia* and pizza snacks are readily available from kiosks, especially those hot from the oven at the kiosk in the exit to Platea Alexandrias. The smaller market cafés provide good value for a quick breakfast or snack. (see box p.15.) Newspapers of all nationalities can be bought under the main gateway onto Mandraki. More sophisticated cafés, with a price to match, line the Mandraki frontage and offer more com-fortable seats but the accom-panying exhaust fumes, noise and crush of people may not be to everyone's taste. On the plus side, the coffee is good and the cakes....! Try the Greek *'ekmet'* which is particularly indulgent and delicious but very different from the original Turkish meaning of the word; bread.

Busy Mandraki Harbour, a name derived from its shape meaning 'sheepfold', is crammed to capacity with sea craft during the summer. Besides use as an international yachting marina, the harbour accommodates local ferry and excursion boats including hydrofoils whilst larger ferries and cruise ships dock in the Commercial Harbour further south. A stroll along the harbour wall past the three windmills, where grain was milled for cargo boats, to **St Nicholas Fort,** now a lighthouse and chapel, provides a clear overview of the waterfront. The view is thwarted somewhat by a forest of bobbing, jangling masts. One of the best vantage points is from the narrow channel at the harbour entrance, especially after 9am when a mass exodus of excursion boats clears the waterfront. Two bronze statues of a stag and doe guard the harbour entrance. The doe replaces a statue of an Italian she-wolf which now resides in the grounds of the Palace of the Grand Masters.

In many ways, Mandraki is the link between the old town and the new. This spacious frontage is where the Italians chose to construct a new commercial quarter. Designed with a mix of Venetian, Gothic and Arabic elements, these monumental public buildings dominate the shoreline. On the seaward side of the road is the **Church of the Evangelist**; built in 1925 on the model of the Knights' Church of St John in the old town which was destroyed in the explosion of 1856. Next to the church is the **Archbishop's Palace** and then the former Governor's Palace, now **Government House** (Nomarkia), constructed in a more photogenic Venetian-Gothic style, whereas a Mussolini square style was used for the Town Hall, Post

Office and **National Theatre**. Fashionable comment derides the tasteless grandeur of these honey-coloured buildings but, they at least provide a better foil for the medieval citadel than the angular mass of soulless concrete they mask.

North of Mandraki, off Platea Koundourioti, is the private **Nautical Club** and the start of the public beach. The coarse sand and shingle beach stretches round the point of Akrotiri Ammou (Sandy Beach) known also as Kumburnu Point. There is plenty of activity on these beaches in summer and changing facilities are available at the Elli Club for a small admission fee. The regimented rows of coloured beach umbrellas, all angled the same way, tell of the persistent breeze along the west coast. Moving west along Papanikolaou, the **Mosque of Murad Reis** watches over a secluded backwater that was once the cemetery for the Turkish elite. Murad Reis himself was a prominent pirate killed during the Turkish siege of 1522 and his tomb is the circular mausoleum next to the mosque. Carved turbans top headstones of men whilst those for women are sharp-angled stone. Despite an air of disuse, a dignified atmosphere still prevails where eucalyptus shade the graves of the many Moslem notables, including a Shah of Persia, which are transformed by carpets of white *Cyclamen persicum* in spring.

Leave this reminder of another age along Sava, in the direction of the sea. Still making for the point along the shoreline, pass the once forlorn Hotel des Roses which is now barely recognisable, by those who remember it, as the now very grand **Rodos Casino**. The **Aquarium**, open 9am - 8.30pm, its more grandiose title being the Hydrobiological Institute, sits in splendid isolation on the northernmost tip of the island and entrance to the subterranean grotto is behind the main building. In an attempt to simulate the seabed, fish found locally are displayed in tanks along the walls of a narrow twisting passageway whilst dried and pickled specimens of swordfish, sharks and a whale can be viewed in separate rooms. A good place to go on a rainy day or to escape the heat.

Now for shopping! (see box p48.) From the Aquarium head directly south through Platea Vas. Pavlou, across Papanikolaou into Grivas. The network of streets between here and Octovriou is the tourist heartland of bars, restaurants and shops. An inelegant collection by day but lively by night! For more upmarket shopping go east along Mandilara to Amerikas then head south. Department stores on Rhodes tend to be compact versions, including Marks & Spencer and BHS. Make for Platea Cyprus down Lambraki, a central point for banks and the more chic establishments. Designer label fashions and shoes sit comfortably alongside discreet and alluring displays of gold. Why umbrellas figure so strongly is a mystery, but there is no shortage of choice from fancy and frivolous to sombre and serviceable. Interspersed between these high-class retailers are some equally stylish cafés. Amongst them Café Central, where it is possible to escape the ubiquitous 'Nes' in favour of filter coffee, espresso or even capuccino and to tempt the palate is a variety of home-made cakes and pastries including 'Xaloumates' (haloumates), a cheese pie made with the less salty Cypriot haloumi cheese and not feta.

The triangle bounded by Averof, Papagou and Platea Cyprus has been pedestrianised, making it very pleasant for browsing or just sitting where a small enclave of Turkish style houses with wooden balconies has been preserved.

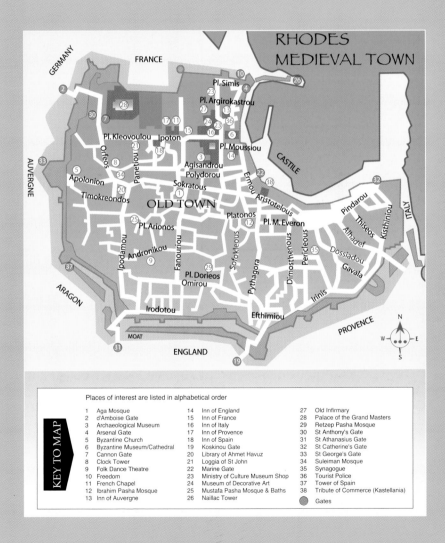

RHODES MEDIEVAL TOWN

Places of interest are listed in alphabetical order

1 Aga Mosque	14 Inn of England	27 Old Infirmary
2 d'Amboise Gate	15 Inn of France	28 Palace of the Grand Masters
3 Archaeological Museum	16 Inn of Italy	29 Retzep Pasha Mosque
4 Arsenal Gate	17 Inn of Provence	30 St Anthony's Gate
5 Byzantine Church	18 Inn of Spain	31 St Athanasius Gate
6 Byzantine Museum/Cathedral	19 Koskinou Gate	32 St Catherine's Gate
7 Cannon Gate	20 Library of Ahmet Havuz	33 St George's Gate
8 Clock Tower	21 Loggia of St John	34 Suleiman Mosque
9 Folk Dance Theatre	22 Marine Gate	35 Synagogue
10 Freedom	23 Ministry of Culture Museum Shop	36 Tourist Police
11 French Chapel	24 Museum of Decorative Art	37 Tower of Spain
12 Ibrahim Pasha Mosque	25 Mustafa Pasha Mosque & Baths	38 Tribute of Commerce (Kastellania)
13 Inn of Auvergne	26 Naillac Tower	◯ Gates

KEY TO MAP

TOUR 4.

MONTE SMITH

A visit to Rhodes Town would not be complete without a trip up the hill of Agios Stefanos, better known as **Monte Smith**, named after the English Admiral Sir Sidney Smith, who kept watch on the Napoleonic fleet from there in 1802. This was the second century BC site of the ancient acropolis, excavated and restored, in part, by the Italians. Very little remains of the once magnificent Temple of Pythian Apollo, but a small Theatre and the Stadium have been restored. Views over the town and across the water to Asia Minor are an unexpected bonus on this trip.

If the 20-30min walk uphill in the heat does not appeal, there is always the tourist train or the regular blue bus which leaves from Mandraki waterfront. Do not forget to buy a prepaid ticket, also one for the return if required, from the kiosk by the bus stop which is validated in the machine on the bus.

From Rimini Square head up Papagou, into Dimokratias then right up Venizelou, signposted **Acropolis of Rhodes**. Follow the signs from here to the large car parking area below the remains. First to catch the eye are the three columns from the Temple of Apollo, re-erected in a somewhat piecemeal fashion and which look better viewed from a distance. The small reconstructed 800 seat Theatre, more likely Odeon, sits beneath the site of the temple. Only the orchestra and three seats remain from the original structure, which was probably used for events associated with the cult of Apollo and maybe by the Rhodian School of Rhetoric. A much larger theatre is thought to have been sited elsewhere on the same hill. On the left is the reconstructed stadium of which again only a few rows, in the middle of the curve, are original. To the east of the stadium lay a Gymnasium but little tangible evidence survives. **The Temple of Apollo** sits on a platform above the huge retaining wall behind the theatre, approached by a flight of steps, and excavations close by are the remains of a fountain house and possible Nymphaia, for the worship of nymphs. To the north, foundations of Temples to Zeus and Athena Polias have been revealed. Return down Voriou Ipirou for spectacular views over the town.

Art Gallery
Open: Mon-Sat 8.00am - 3.00pm.
Closed Sunday.

Aquarium
Subterranean display of local fish and also preserved specimens.
Open: Daily 9.00am - 8.30pm in summer.

Archaeological Museum
Mycenaean to Roman exhibits.
Open: Tues-Sun 8.30am -7pm (closes earlier in winter). Closed Monday.

Byzantine Museum. Panagia Kastrou Exhibition
Byzantine & Post-Byzantine Ikons.
Open: Tues-Sun 8.30am - 3.00pm.
Closed Monday.

Greek Folk Dances by Nelly Dimoglou
Traditional Greek Dances.
7 Andronikou
Mon, Wed, Fri only from 9.20pm - 11.00pm. May - Oct.

Ministry of Culture shop
Rhodes old town
Open 8am - 2.30pm, closed Sunday and holidays

Monte Smith
Temple of Apollo, Ancient Stadium & Theatre.
Open access.

Museum of Decorative Arts
Folklore exhibits from Dodecanese Islands.
Open: Tues-Sun 8.30am - 3.00pm.
Closed Monday.

Palace of the Grand Masters
Open: Tues-Sun 8.30am - 7.00pm.
Closed Monday.

Son et Lumiére
English language times.
Mon & Tues. 8.15pm; Weds, Fri & Sat.

9.15pm; Thurs. 10.15pm. Summer only.

To Rolio - The Clock Tower
Open daily in season

Turkish Baths
Platea Arionos
Men: Monday, Wednesday, Friday
Women: Tuesday, Thursday, Saturday
Open: 11am - 6pm weekdays and 8am - 6pm Saturday

Turkish Library of Ahmet Havuz
Open 9.30am - 4pm, closed Sunday

Walk Around the Walls
Starts from the Palace of the Grand Masters every Tuesday and Saturday at 2.45pm.

Transport

Buses:
There is an excellent bus service on Rhodes providing connections to most towns and villages on the island. There is a full listing of bus times and destinations in the free paper, Rodos News, available in the Tourist Office.

Buy tickets before boarding the bus at the kiosk.

Taxis:

Taxi fares to and from Rhodes town are listed and clearly displayed at the main taxi rank in Rhodes town. They are also listed in the free paper, Rodos News, available from the Tourist Office

Tourist mini-train: Rhodes Town

Starts at the National Theatre and runs hourly from 10.30am - 1.30pm and 5.30 - 8.30pm

Boats and Hydrofoils

Daily excursions and ferries to other islands and Piraeus. Check travel agencies for details.

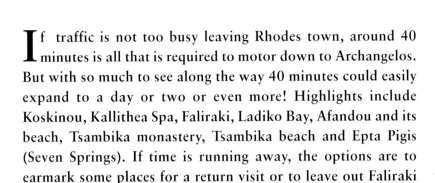

If traffic is not too busy leaving Rhodes town, around 40 minutes is all that is required to motor down to Archangelos. But with so much to see along the way 40 minutes could easily expand to a day or two or even more! Highlights include Koskinou, Kallithea Spa, Faliraki, Ladiko Bay, Afandou and its beach, Tsambika monastery, Tsambika beach and Epta Pigis (Seven Springs). If time is running away, the options are to earmark some places for a return visit or to leave out Faliraki and Koskinou which can easily be visited by bus.

Leave Rhodes town following signs to Faliraki and Lindos. There are two routes out of town both signposted Faliraki, one following closely by the coast and the other taking a more inland route. Follow the inland route by turning right at the junction where Faliraki is indicated both to the right and straight on. The suburbs of Rhodes town have little to attract attention although this road passes **Rodini Park** on the right which once had deer but now just has peacocks to entertain visitors. Once through Asgourou, look for a signposted left turn to **Koskinou** which is located just after a short section of dual carriageway. Perched on the top of a steep escarpment, the village soon comes into view and is reached after 2km (1 1/4 miles). There is plenty of parking near the large church in the centre. Unfortunately, the church is usually locked so, unless there is a service in progress, it is not usually possible to look around.

Koskinou village is a maize of narrow, rambling streets crowded by traditional Rhodian homes with plant filled courtyards. The courtyards are mostly enclosed by large ornamental gateways, some very grand with arched doorways guarded by embedded ionic columns bearing an ornate entablature. It is one of only a few villages on the island which has made no concessions to tourism and has retained an old way of life. If you can find Yannis' taverna in the narrow streets, it is worth remembering the location. Only open in the evening, it serves excellent traditional Greek food and is well worth a return trip. Do not expect peppered steaks but if there is a party of four, try the *mezedes* and watch the table being filled with a whole range of Greek dishes and at very reasonable cost. Two people on their own simply end up with a smaller selection.

The expansion of Koskinou for tourists' needs has taken place

2.5km (1 1/2 miles) away down by the coast. Leave the village heading east to find it. It is mainly a collection of hotels and tavernas but there is a beach. On meeting the main coast road, turn left and very shortly right into the road signposted Eden Roc Hotel. A dirt road on the left 200m (yds) leads down to the beach but it is best to leave the car at the top. It is a fair sized, sandy beach with limited water sports facilities.

Return to the main road where self-caterers might decide to turn right to stock up at the large Spar supermarket just down the road; here prices are much keener than in the small supermarkets, otherwise turn left to head south.

Turn left to **Thermal Kallithea** (Thermai Kallithea), after 4km (2.5 miles), opposite a bow-fronted domed ruin on the right. The spa entrance is a little way down this road where there is a café-bar by the entrance and plenty of space for parking outside. There is no entrance fee for the spa.

This area has been famous for its spa water since antiquity but the present Moorish style buildings were constructed by the Italians around 1920. The lavish circular and domed buildings are set around a rocky inlet with a scattering of palm trees adding a touch of the exotic. Immediately through the entrance, a huge circular fountain sets the tone. Beyond, a grand Moorish arch, one of many, marks the entrance to a colonnade which leads down to the main spa building. The floor of the colonnade set with black and white pebbles is a fine example of the Rhodian art of *hochlaki* which is mostly seen in houses or courtyards. The black and white pebbles are set in patterns, sometimes geometric but often with floral or other motifs like the Byzantine eagle.

The circular domed building at the foot of the steps is where the waters were taken. Whatever ailments these waters cured, and they were good for the liver, the kidney and rheumatism, the effect on the bladder was dramatic judging by the number of toilets in the adjacent building. Simply follow the path off to the right towards another circular building. This huge toilet block is in a dismal state but a walk around the outside gives a good impression of how it was originally. Back in the main area, there is a beach which is used for sunbathing as are the rocks and pathway alongside the inlet where the mature palm trees act as sun umbrellas. There is another beach, **Nikolas beach**, lying adjacent to the spa to the south. It is a well

Church tower, Koskinou

furnished beach too with sun beds and umbrellas, boardwalks over the sand with a bar/restaurant on hand.

Return to the coast road and turn left for the 5.7km (3.6 mile) run to **Faliraki**. Very shortly the road closes with the coast and the whole sweep of Faliraki bay stretches out into the distance. The northern end of this beach is least attractive in sand quality but hotel development is spreading to this area and a short distance along the hotels are suddenly all large and flourishing. Although still 2-3km (1.25-1.9 miles) from Faliraki centre, this is hotel land where the impressive **water park** is found on the right and where the great majority of the resort's hotels are situated. Those on the coastal side mostly have access to the beach behind. Where the hotels are replaced by shops and tavernas, Faliraki is close and when the junction is reached turn left down the main street and again at the roundabout near the beach to find a parking place.

Faliraki is a resort which tries to be all things to all people. In reality it is two resorts in one, a family resort by day and the liveliest hotspot on the island by night. In spite of the resort's poor image, almost all the evening's noisy nightlife centres around one or two main streets in the centre and is easily avoided.

By day, Faliraki is just another family resort with a beautiful beach. If in search of activities, just about everything is there to be found, water sports in variety, water slides, go-kart racing, football competitions, bungee jumping or even snake watching at the **snake farm**. If the evening arrives and you still have energy to spare, there is always the **Luna Park**, open 7pm-1am May to October, where you can enjoy all the non-stop fun of the fair. Shoppers can shop to their heart's content from designer labels down to the standard tourist trivia. It is not too surprising that the criticism mostly uttered is that it is brash and noisy and it is, in parts. The main street, all tourist shops and supermarkets by day transforms at night. When the bars open it throbs with all the heat of a sore thumb. Every step down the road meets decibels of jungle beat reinforced here and there where the cacophony from nearby bars overlap. It takes a real artisan to know the music has actually changed! The youngsters love it and head there in droves during the evening. Trouble is not unknown and this is not the place to be for a woman on her own late at night. But this is only one or two streets and easily avoided if it is not to taste.

As always, there is another side and it is still possible to enjoy a more peaceful holiday. High density building is not a feature of the resort, quite the opposite. Faliraki covers a large area and, apart from hotel land on the northern edge, much of the accommodation is low rise rooms and apartments which are scattered around still with plenty of space between. It has also spread west of the main road in the direction of Kalithies. So there is quieter accommodation to be found and all the outlying areas are well served

Good Beach Guide

All the best beaches on Rhodes are generally found down the east coast of the island. West coast visitors have to manage with narrow shingle beaches and a constant wind. The Mistral, which blows steadily from the north throughout the summer, affects the west coast far more than the east but the beach umbrellas are set at an angle to offer sunbathers shelter. In the full heat of summer, the wind actually makes the temperatures more bearable but in early season it can be a nuisance. Apart from Ixia and Trianda, all the main resorts on the island lie on or near the east coast. Both Ixia and Trianda have good, if narrow beaches with excellent services and plenty of water sports.

From north to south on the east coast:

Faliraki offers a 6km, almost 4 mile stretch of sandy beach. Very popular and busy, especially the central part, it is good for swimming and there is a full range of water sports and activities available from para-gliding to bungee jumping. It has just about every facility available; bars, tavernas, snacks as well as beach furniture and showers. Those who prefer things a little quieter should head for the two smaller bays at the south end.

Ladiko is a tiny, intimate bay with only a small beach but a great atmosphere. There are a few sun beds with umbrellas and a taverna.

Afandou offers another enormous stretch of beach, this time largely shingle. Usually possible to find a few acres of space all to yourself. Very few facilities but there are three tavernas to the south. The sea here is always edged a milky blue.

Scenic Tsambika beach is the place to write your name in the sand, possibly the best on the island. Bounded by headlands and overlooked by Tsambika monastery, this bay of fine sand is a beauty spot which thankfully has not attracted the developers. It is good for swimming but there are only limited facilities which include sun loungers and canteens. It is only accessible by car or by foot which helps to keep it from becoming too crowded.

Agathi beach lies just to the north of Haraki. It is an intimate and delightful stretch of sandy beach backed, unfortunately, by some unfinished developments started more than a decade ago. The gently shelving beach makes it good for children. Limited facilities in season.

Lindos, overlooked by the Acropolis, is another beach of great natural

Left inset: *Faliraki beach* **Below inset:** *Ladiko beach*

beauty. It is no secret so prepare to share with a lot of other sunbathers. Good facilities and some water sports.

Pefkos has some interesting if small beaches and is itself an expanding tourist development. Facilities increase almost yearly and there are plenty of snack bars and tavernas.

Lardos is another expanding resort with plenty of beach in Lardos Bay. The village and beach are well separated but hotels are springing up in the bay. Good quality sand and plenty of activities.

Glystra is a small beach visible from the road south of Lardos. Picturesque but with limited facilities which includes sun beds.

Plimmiri has a large sweep of coarse sand looking like something from the South Pacific but with no facilities except a taverna.

Prasonissi is perched out at the very southern tip of the island and is connected only by a wide sandspit. Very picturesque with the sea approaching from both sides. To the west the sea is usually rough with breakers and to the east calm, but not always. A favourite spot for windsurfers, surfers and all sports involving the wind and the sea. Accommodation and tavernas on hand.

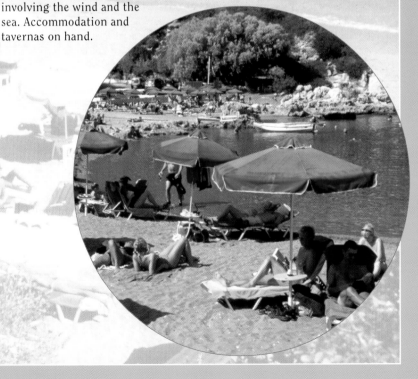

by tavernas. The beach remains the major feature and the resort still attracts families with children. Good escapes from the crowds are found in the smaller bays at the south end of the resort where there are restaurants and tavernas overlooking the beach.

Eating in Faliraki is not always the pleasure it should be. The fare in most tavernas has moved away from traditional dishes to suit international tastes and, with a constantly changing customer base, trouble to do neither very well. Since Faliraki has few resident Greeks, they all live in nearby Kalithies, watching where the Greeks eat is no help. For good basic Greek food, Yannis' taverna O Kantas at the south part of the town near Hotel Luka Faliraki is worth seeking out.

The main street is one way for traffic so return to the main road by continuing across the roundabout in a southerly direction then heading inland at the first opportunity. On reaching the main road by Asda supermarket turn left. If finding Asda is a surprise then Tesco, Sainsburys, Safeways and Morrisons too raise eyebrows but all these names have simply been hijacked and they have no connection to any major supermarket chain.

Once on the main road the Ladiko junction on the left is reached in a minute. Turn left here and keep ahead. Stay left at the fork shortly reached but stay right next to head down into **Ladiko bay**. Here, headlands enclose a clear blue sea in a most intimate and picturesque manner. Little moves except for fishermen straightening their yellow nets although tourist boats sometimes anchor offshore to enjoy the swimming. Languid sunbathers using the facilities on the small sandy beach seem infected by the tranquillity moving only to the taverna at the rear when hunger

Water Park - Faliraki

Here is a park with just about everything for all the family! Owned by the same company who run the Luna Park (Fantasia) fairground in the centre of Faliraki, a full range of facilities which include a supermarket, souvenir shop, train and a choice of cafés/bars is on site.

The fun element includes 11 thrilling slides which have challenging titles such as Space Ball, Free Fall, Kamikaze, Turbo and Black Hole. A Pirate's Ship, Wave Pool, Aqua Gym and Tarzan Pool are just another selection of the 22 attractions on offer.

To find the Water Park, head along the coast road in the direction of Rhodes Town for around 3km and it is on the left. The Water Park, like the Luna Park, is open May - October. Gates open at 9.30am - 6pm. Children under 3 are free and under 12s are charged a little over half price, if under 1.5m in height, otherwise they pay the full adult price. Check out the site at www.info@water-park.gr

or thirst demands it.

The '**Anthony Quinn**' bay, where the Guns of Navarone was filmed, lies just to the north. The road on the right just up from Ladiko beach leads to it, although you will have to park at the top of the hill. There is a taverna/snack bar and sunbeds available for this piece of rocky shoreline, enough to attract the sunbathers.

Return to the main road and continue south. Afandou Bay sweeping away to a backdrop of mountains is one of the islands most breathtaking views. One of those tricks of perspective presents the four individual and characteristic mountain peaks as a continuous range while in reality they are well separated in space. The inland peak guards Kolimbia Junction, the flat-topped one to the left overlooks Archangelos and the two on the seaward side are on the

headland at Tsambika.

Just 3km (1.9 miles) after joining the main road, turn left down by the golf course to reach **Afandou beach**. This 18-hole golf course is the only one on the island. The long, long stretch of beach is mainly sand and pebbles edged by a sea of the most startling milky-blue. A slow enrichment of the beach is in hand as machines are used here to separate off the pebbles for aggregate while returning the sand to the beach. Holiday accommodation is slowly growing a little way back from the beach but for most of the time it is very quiet. Sun beds and umbrellas are few but drinks and food are available from tavernas at the southern end. The masts and aerials at the extreme south end belong to a radio station which broadcasts the Voice of America.

Afandou is reached by taking the road from around the centre of the

Anthony Quinn bay

beach and driving inland, crossing above the main coastal road on a flyover. It is a case of parking where you can in the centre. With a population of 5,677, Afandou is the second largest village on the island after Ialysos. Apricots contribute towards its economy and hand made carpets once played a large part but less so now. Bustling about its daily business, the village seems to ignore tourism but there is an increasing amount of accommodation with all the dependent tavernas and services.

Return by the same road towards the flyover but this time filter right down the slip road just before to rejoin the main coastal road again heading south. There is a mere 4.2km (2.6miles) to travel, hardly chance to relax and enjoy the scenery, before Kolimbia junction is reached and the road to Epta Pigis on the right. The tour in Chapter 7 also passes Epta Pigis so if time is pressing, it can be left out now and included

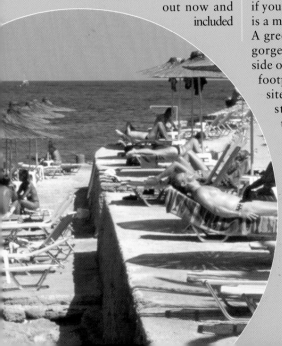

later. Looking at the bare stony fields at the start of this road inland, it is hard to imagine that they are full of wild orchids in the early spring. The pink butterfly, *Orchis papilionacea,* is particularly common here. Open pine forest offers the first hint of verdancy before the junction for the **Seven Springs** (Epta Pigis) is reached after just 3km (1.9miles). Turn left and head up to the car park. Alternatively, there is a pleasant woodland walk, about 10 minutes, from the junction which takes you to the heart of this beauty spot. Park here, if the coaches leave some space, enter the road for the Seven Springs but take the path on the right immediately and follow through the woodland.

The scent of pine on every breath, dappled sunlight, rustic bridges and trickling streams set the mood for Epta Pigis. It is no problem finding the seven springs, they all lie close to the taverna but, if you wish to wander further, there is a maize of footpaths to discover. A green lake nestles in a pine clad gorge and is found on the other side of the entry road. A signposted footpath leads to it from the main site as does a tunnel carrying a stream. Many people walk through the 186m (200yds) dark tunnel but it can be dangerous when the water is racing or on emerging at the lake where it slopes steeply. Peacocks wander the site too and if they are not to be seen their penetrating cry is unlikely to pass unnoticed. Set in some of the deepest shade

Opposite inset: Sunbathing around Kallithea spa
Above: *The magnificent view south from Tsambika Monastery*
Below: *Efta Pigis*

by the waters edge, the taverna is an atmospheric place to refresh and the food is good too. Before tourism, the Italians harnessed the waters of the Seven Springs to irrigate the orange groves around Kolimbia.

Name That Church

The countryside sometimes seems littered with small, mostly white churches. No matter how simple, each one has a name which can be worked out from the ikons contained within. It is fun to try and challenging even with these guidelines. Knowing the Greek alphabet helps for identifying the saints but when ancient script is used, it can be even more difficult.

If the doorway in the ikonostasis is central, then the ikon of the Virgin Mary should be on the left and the ikon of the saint after which the church is named to the left of the Virgin Mary. Christ is on the right of the doorway and St John the Baptist to the right of Christ.

If the doorway is not central, it is usually on the left taking up the space normally reserved for the ikon dedicated to the saint of the church. Now, the ikon of the saint to which the church is dedicated is then placed on the right of Christ.

It works most of the time but there are still pitfalls to watch out for, especially when the church is dedicated to two or more saints.

Return by the same route to Kolimbia junction on the main coastal road and cross directly over to head into **Kolimbia**. Once around the church, an avenue deeply shaded by mature eucalyptus trees runs straight as a die for 2km (1.25 miles) across the plain towards the sea.

Kolimbia, once all agriculture and fishing, is a rapidly developing purpose built resort constructed on the usual Greek scatter plan which may come together eventually. The avenue acts as the centre where most of the shops are to be found and around, mainly to the south, is an extravagantly laid out grid system of roads. To the left from the end of the road lies a small fishing harbour with tavernas and beyond is a good beach furnished with sun beds and umbrellas where some water sports are available. Boat excursions also leave from here. To the right is the fishermen's bay enclosed by a spit and beyond a taverna. A right turn just before the end of the road leads to another large sandy beach looked over by Tsambika monastery. With an uncrowded feel, it is an ideal place for a quiet beach holiday.

Turn left back at the main coast road to head for the next port of call, **Tsambika Monastery**. The road up to the monastery is just 1.7km (1 mile) further on and, although signposted (also Panoramic Restaurant), its narrow entrance is easily missed. This narrow concrete road winds steeply up the mountainside stopping short of the monastery in a small car parking area just beyond the taverna. Unfortunately, there is still

Savas Pottery

Rhodes has a long history of pottery going back many centuries at least to the time of the ancient cities. The island has many keramic factories selling hand painted pottery, typically vases, plates and ash trays. Vivid colours, especially blue, feature strongly as do certain motifs which are uniquely Rhodian, the pomegranate flower and the stylised deer. Some factories also make copies of pottery found on the island's ancient sites but none better than Savas.

This family run a true cottage industry. Outside on the potters wheel, Savas' son can sometimes be seen throwing pots or will demonstrate. Inside his mother painstakingly hand paints the pottery with patience and admirable skill. Also outside is the brick built, wood fired kiln which is no longer used now but was until fairly recently.

Firing the kiln, stacked full with many shelves of pots, was an art in itself. First the doorway was bricked up and the fire started with large pieces of wood. As the bottom of the kiln started to warm, smaller pieces of wood were added to encourage the flames higher followed by finer pieces to ensure that the heat reached the highest parts. Using the skills and experience passed down through the generations, the uniform high temperature required for a successful firing was routinely achieved. Cooling was another low-tec highly skilled process. Bricks were taken out of the kiln walls at strategic points as required. The biscuit fired pottery which emerged was then ready for hand painting, predominantly in hues of orange and brown

Their speciality is replicas of ancient pottery found on the island and a seventeenth-century B.C. wine vessel or similar can be carried away at absolutely give-away prices. They are open every day in the middle of summer but only Tuesday and Friday afternoons at quieter times.

Replica museum pieces, a speciality of Savas pottery   69

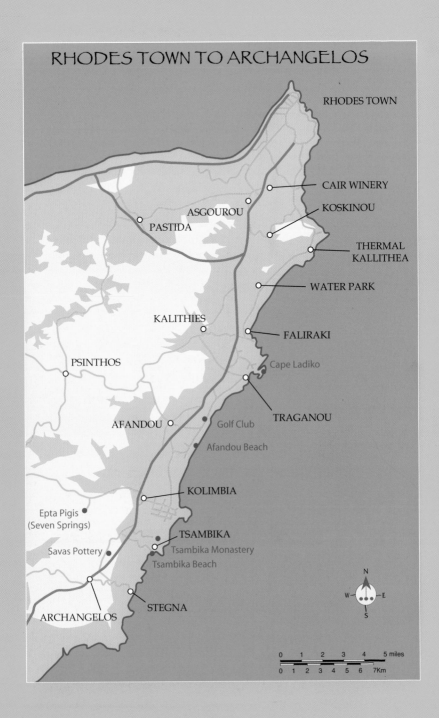

RHODES TOWN TO ARCHANGELOS

RHODES TOWN

CAIR WINERY

KOSKINOU

ASGOUROU

PASTIDA

THERMAL
KALLITHEA

WATER PARK

KALITHIES

FALIRAKI

Cape Ladiko

PSINTHOS

TRAGANOU

AFANDOU   Golf Club

Afandou Beach

KOLIMBIA

Epta Pigis
(Seven Springs)

TSAMBIKA

Savas Pottery   Tsambika Monastery

Tsambika Beach

N
W   E
S

STEGNA

ARCHANGELOS

0   1   2   3   4   5 miles
0 1 2 3 4 5 6 7Km

Right inset & below: Archangelos, the beautiful 'wedding cake' church tower
Bottom: Fresco of St George inside the tiny chapel in the castle grounds

some distance to climb on foot with plenty of steps, 297 in all to reach the church, but there is a good paved way to follow.

Tsambika Monastery is a tiny white Byzantine church perched high at 300m (985ft) with commanding coastal views both north over Kolimbia where the avenue of eucalyptus trees can be picked out and the grid layout appreciated and south over Tsambika beach and beyond to distant Lindos. Inside is the miraculous 11th-century ikon of the Blessed Virgin found on the mountain by a childless, infertile couple who later conceived a child. The legend is that if a childless woman wishing to conceive walks barefoot up the mountain to pray to the Virgin, she will be blessed with children. Children so inspired are named after the monastery, Tsambikos for a boy and Tsambika for a girl, a name unique to Rhodes. It is so common on the island, it is more likely that fertile women named their offspring after the monastery by way of thanks that it had not been necessary to undergo this ritual. The saint's day is September 7th, an especially potent occasion for the infertile.

Tsambika beach is easily reached by returning to the coastal road, heading south and taking the first left. There is plenty of space behind the beach for parking and even for a barbecue if organised. Enclosed by Tsambika's hill perched on the north side and a sandbank of a headland to the south, this beach of fine sand is as natural and inviting as they come. Facilities, although limited to a couple of small shops and café bars, are enough to ensure that a day can be lazed away beneath a sun umbrella without having to stir too far for sustenance.

On returning to the main road go directly across to join part of the old National road. It is only a 4.5km (2.8 miles) stretch but a very scenic run through olive groves. Turn left at the T junction and it is up and away over the hills. The cluster of white buildings with a wind pump on the descent is **Savas pottery**. All the stages of pot making and painting can usually be seen here in a friendly atmosphere totally devoid of sales pressure.

On leaving the Savas pottery, continue on to meet the main coast road, turn left and immediately right to head into **Archangelos**. Follow into the centre and park on the left immediately by the bridge over the river.

With 4,170 residents, Archangelos is one of the larger settlements on the island. At first sight, the modern centre sprawling beneath the medieval Crusader castle appears to have nothing to offer, apart from bars and tavernas, but the old town has plenty: white houses in narrow streets, brightly coloured gateways, blossoms trailing from painted cans, traditional houses and the wedding-cake white **Church of Archangel Michael** which gives the town its name. Thigh-length leather boots, snake protectors, which can be folded down in stages once filled the shoe shops. Snakes must be less of a problem as these boots are only made to order now but pairs are occasionally seen on display. Hand made carpets and ceramics are the town's specialities.

Wander into the main square and then left heading up towards the castle. Built by the Crusaders under Grand Master Orsini in 1467 as part of a chain of defences against the Turks, (see the feature on p.108), the renovated outer walls are the only significant remains. Tucked away inside, occupying a corner position, is a little white church dedicated to St George. If the little old lady in black is around then it is almost obligatory to step inside and admire the modern fresco of St George slaying the dragon.

Looking down on the town from here, the icing sugar tower of the main church is easily picked out, finding a route down to it through the maze of narrow streets is a different matter. It lies at the heart of the old town crowded in by houses. The wedding-cake style of church tower is commonly seen on this island and others in the Dodecanese group but this one at Archangelos is one of the prettiest. Cross vaulting, instead of the more usual barrel vault, is also a feature of church architecture on the island. Just outside the main entrance of the church, on the left when departing, there is a fine example of an old traditional house (see feature on p.96). If the traditional old lady in black sitting outside offers an invitation, take it! It is too good to miss.

Additional Information

Places to Visit

Thermal Kallithea

Italianate spa
Open: every day, daylight hours, no admission charge.

Epta Pigis

Beauty spot
Open site, no admission charge.

Snake Farm, Faliraki

Reptile house
Open: every day, 11.00am-11.00pm.

The coastal region between Archangelos and Lindos is largely used for agriculture, especially so around Malona. Here citrus groves fill much of the countryside and the old National road which leads from Archangelos through Malona and Massari goes right through the heart of them. In April, with the scent of orange blossom on every breath, it is unthinkable not to use this route. The successful culture of oranges demands good summer irrigation and there is plenty of opportunity to judge the results in early season. Orange trees with either blossom or fruit on the trees all year round are never without interest but the harvest season is early, from January through to May depending on the variety. Farmers set up stalls alongside the main road and arrange colourful and eye-catching displays to attract trade from passing motorists. Neither Malona nor Massari have much to attract visitors except the ambience of a working Greek village. Old men relaxing in tavernas idly tormenting their worry beads whilst watching the tractors trundle through sort of atmosphere. In contrast to all the greenness of this area, Lindos is barren with barely any land for cultivation. Vines were grown there up to a few years ago but the wines they made were not of the best quality so they have now been rooted out.

If the diversion through Malona is not followed, use the good fast road from Archangelos to Lindos for a quick 20km (12.5 miles) run. There are a couple of side trips on the way, one to Stegna Bay and the other to Feraklos castle, Agathi beach and Haraki, these last three lie close together. At the end of the journey awaits Lindos. With its white cubic houses clustered on the slopes below a fortified acropolis, Lindos is one of the most breathtaking sights in the Aegean. It is also one of those places which runs away with time. There is a case to argue for arriving early to beat the crowds. Just about every coach on the island visits every day but later on Monday, when the Acropolis opens only lunchtime. Coaches seldom arrive before 9.30

am on most days. The usual pattern is for disgorged tourists to head up first to the Acropolis, explore the town then flock back to the coach and on to the next stop. The Acropolis opens early around, 8am, so there is a good hour or so for a leisurely inspection free of jostle for independent travellers.

There is a good footpath through the countryside down to **Stegna** for those who prefer to walk, see the feature box p.77. For car drivers it takes only a few moments. Follow the signposted road on the left just over the bridge from the parking place and fork left very shortly. The route is straight on at the next junction reached after 1km (0.6 miles) but note that the road joining from the left here is the intended return to the main road. Stegna is quickly reached. A road leads around the bay passing a selection of tavernas and giving glimpses of clusters of fishermen's cottages which are slowly being swamped by modern buildings. The sandy shingle beach stretches around the bay with enough facilities to make it look interesting and attractive.

On leaving Stegna by the same route, take the first road off right and turn left on reaching the main coast road for the 7km (4.4 mile) journey down to the Haraki junction. Again turn left on a good road towards the coast. Ignore the first turn off left signposted Agathi beach but take the second turn which gives access to both Feraklos castle and Agathi beach.

Agathi beach can be reached from the castle by continuing along the track. Skeletal buildings of an unfinished development at the rear spoils the ambience but it does not detract when actually on the beach. Expect a beach of excellent sand and some supporting services in the way of café bars. Across the far side of the beach is the tiny church of Ag. Agathi built into a cave.

Feraklos castle, another medieval castle, was actually used by pirates before the Knights of St John ousted them, reinforced the castle then used it as a prison. Reached from the track by a footpath leading to steps, it is a good climb and fairly rough underfoot. Make a mental note of the entry point into the castle since this is much less obvious on the return. Like many of these fortifications on the island, the walls are the only significant remains. This one is no exception and the inside is overgrown with shrubs and other vegetation. Narrow footpaths lead around the enclosure and there are excellent views from the walls down to Agathi beach and to Haraki in the other direction.

Return along the track to the road and turn left to **Haraki**. There is a car park along the road to the right before reaching the sea front.

Separated from the main sweep of beach running south by a headland, Haraki nestles around its own intimate bay. Originally a small fishing hamlet, only a handful of the original fishermen's cottages are still to be seen clustered near the headland, it has developed into a small settlement. A promenade divides the single ribbon of low rise houses, apartments and shops from the shingle beach. The exclusion of traffic adds tranquillity to the

Archangelos to Stegna Bay on foot

Some of this walk is over stony footpaths through the countryside so that good footwear is essential. The return distance is around 8km (5 miles) so allow 1 hour each way. It is best to make a few mental notes on the outward leg since the return is by the same route or by the road (3km) if preferred.

Set out from the bridge in Archangelos initially following the road signposted to Stegna. Where the Stegna road forks left in 2 minutes, keep right. Continue ahead as the road reverts to track. Olive groves soften an otherwise barren landscape at this point and, looking back, there are good views of the old castle above Archangelos. In around 17min, be ready to fork left onto a minor stony track, where the main track bends more right. This track rises initially before starting to descend towards Stegna Bay where it becomes concreted briefly. At this point, there is a view of Tsambika Monastery on its hill over to the left. Ignore a minor track off left into olive groves a minute down this track and stay ahead when a rising track forks left soon afterwards. Keep an eye open now for a red waymarked path forking down right.

Turn right to continue the descent along this waymarked path. In a few minutes, the path leads along the right edge of a gulley where the going becomes particularly stony and rocky but a slower pace allows more time to appreciate the fine scenery. No matter how dry and arid the ground here looks in summer, it is well decorated with flowers in early season, especially with the showy red turban buttercup, **Ranunculus asiaticus**. Views of Stegna Bay are particularly good from this vantage point. Once out of the gulley, the path leads around to the right above Stegna Bay and continues south, parallel with the bay, before dropping down to the coast. Follow the path which leads along the inland edge of an olive grove then crosses it diagonally left. Continue in the same direction on the seaward side of the olive grove. The path runs into a rough field track along the top edge of a plateau above Stegna, which is down to the left, heading towards a blue and white house on the same level. Before reaching the house, descend left to join a dirt track which leads to meet a concrete track just before the house. Turn left along the concrete track which soon heads down into Stegna Bay to emerge by the port. There are plenty of facilities in season all along the road behind the beach. To return along the road, head to the far end of Stegna.

Stegna Bay

cosiness. It has a great atmosphere for eating and Thalassa (The Sea) taverna on the front offers good Greek food but for something more upmarket Argo restaurant on the headland is the place, especially for fish.

Return to the main coastal road and turn south for the final run to Lindos. **Kalathos** comes first which boasts the luxurious Atrium Palace Hotel, tucked away on the seaward side. It looks over to a sandy shingle beach which is steadily being enriched with the addition of more sand. Keep ahead at the Lardos junction or turn left for a quick diversion down to **Vlicha Bay**. This is another developing resort with two large hotels and some smaller ones looking on to a fairly good sandy beach. These are the nearest large hotels to Lindos.

Be prepared to stop as **Lindos** comes into view. There is a view point with a large pull off on the left. From here the view is the

inspiration of poets, painters and photographers. Golden sand edges a violet limpid pool in the horseshoe bay, white houses are scattered in a dense ribbon on the hillside, each one snuggled against the next safely in the shadow and protection of the fortified **Acropolis** standing sentinel on the flat-topped hill above. It is a view which has persuaded more than one visitor that there can be no finer place on earth to live. Lawrence Durrell described Lindos as ' of a scrupulous Aegean order, and perfect of its kind'.

Parking can be a little problematic in the middle of the day. There is a large car parking area ahead just beyond the left turn down into the town. A shuttle bus runs from here to the centre in season or it entails a short walk downhill. There are lay-bys a little further down the road into Lindos, which fill up early, and further parking on the road to the beach and at the end of that road. Tourist traffic is not allowed in the main square at the bottom of the hill, except for turning and there is usually police traffic control directing everybody to the left along the beach road. For easier access into Lindos itself, continue ahead past the first turning into Lindos and head towards **St Paul's Bay**. There is parking at the bay and a car park along to the left close to the entrance to the village.

The square is as near to the village as traffic is allowed since the narrow streets were laid out long

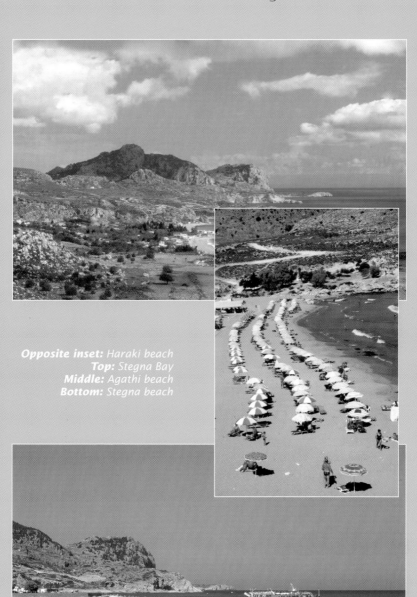

Opposite inset: Haraki beach
Top: Stegna Bay
Middle: Agathi beach
Bottom: Stegna beach

before the invention of motorised vehicles and more with the donkey in mind. Many of the houses in the village have been converted to tourist accommodation and moving luggage around is done by small three-wheeled pickups, probably converted from motorbikes, which chug along the narrow streets. Tourists arriving at night often have to part with their luggage in the main square and await its delivery the next morning! Lindos is under the protection of the Greek Archaeological Society which is concerned with the preservation of the village and only allows development which is totally in sympathy with the present structures. Despite these limitations, new developments are taking place expanding the village in the direction of St Paul's Bay. Typically, white cubic rooms and apartments are built around a small courtyard with just one door opening to the street.

Even though Lindos is a magnet for tourism and the coaches pile in one after the other, the narrow streets soon absorb and disperse the crowds. Few day trippers have time to spare beyond the obligatory acropolis visit and a look at the beach. For them it is a quick tour and away. The main thoroughfares are covered for shade and colourfully decked with tourist trappings, T-shirts, carpets, post cards, and racks of souvenirs. Here also are the bars, tavernas and eateries of all description. Most of them tucked away well out of sight and some in the most delightful settings. Doorways open to courtyard cafés, like Gelo Blu with its home made ice cream and

Lindos: on foot to an inland viewpoint

There is a short walk out of Lindos into the interior countryside leading up to a fine viewpoint which gives a wholly different perspective of Lindos. The impregnability of the huge monolith which bears the acropolis can more readily be appreciated. Similar shaped rocks occur at Feraklos and Monolithos and both of those have been converted into strongholds.

Good shoes, at least trainers, are suggested since this walk is partly over stony ground. Allow around 1 hour for the return trip from the car park at the top of the hill.

From the car park follow south down the road towards Pefkos. Almost immediately, just past bus parking and Super Market 'Flora' turn right along a narrow surfaced road. Stay ahead, ignoring tracks/roads off. The road reverts to track before bending around to the left. Before it bends left again, look for a strong path heading up the hillside to the right which is marked by stone cairns. Follow the path as it winds first up the bank and then through the field to reach a hillside. Carry on following the path until the crest of the hill is reached which is the viewpoint.

The Lindian Archondiko

The Lindian mansion (*archondiko*) is unique to Lindos. Dress, customs, language and architecture all reflect this city's individuality evolving from

a long history and commercial success over many centuries. From the beginning of the seventeenth century through to the nineteenth century, archondika were built from the wealth of ship owners and captains but the most grand and richly decorated were those of the early period. The architecture draws on elements from the Byzantine, medieval and Arab influences to create an individuality which is purely Lindian. Many of the early archondika are still in good condition and still occupied. Later mansions showed the more contemporary influences with the addition of a second storey and elements of neo-classicism.

The best features in the island's own style of architecture were not ignored and central to the *archondiko* was a courtyard decorated with hochlaki, black and white sea pebbles with motifs sometimes reflecting the source of their wealth, fish and ships etc., or drawn from Byzantine art. Separated from the street by a high wall, a heavily decorated door (the pylionas) with an arched or horizontal lintel gave access to the courtyard. Around the sides of the courtyards, usually right and left of the pylionas, were the utility rooms, namely the kitchen, the oven, the stables, the toilet and maybe even a special room for an olive press. At the rear of the courtyard, opposite the pylionas, was the entertaining room, the sala, which was often the largest room in the house. The inner room was fitted with raised platforms for sleeping as described for the traditional house (p. 96) except they were more lavishly decorated with carvings. All the inner floors were constructed with pebbles.

Another characteristic of the Lindian *archondiko* was the 'Captain's' room which can be traced back in prototype form to the time of the Knights of St John. This was usually located above the pylionas, or occasionally over the street and accessed by stairs from the courtyard. It was small compared with the sala but had many windows opening to the street, unlike the rest of the house. Outside, the façade and the door were richly decorated with cable patterns in relief and the lintel above the door usually bore a cross.

Top inset: *Lindos looking from the south*
Above: *Lindos looking from the north*

The Acropolis of Lindos

The enduring success of Lindos is almost directly attributable to a triangular flat-topped outcrop of rock, 116m (380ft) high, which juts out

into the sea creating two natural harbours and presenting an easily defended stronghold. History traces occupation of this site back as far as the Neolithic Age (2500 - 2000 BC) but, although findings suggest Mycenaean occupation, is was not until around the tenth century BC that Lindos rose to great prominence along with the other two cities of antiquity on the island, Kamiros and Ialyssos. A temple dedicated to Athena Lindia has existed on this rock from at least this period.

Kleoboulos, who governed the city for 40 years in the sixth century BC, ruled moderately and wisely and drew great respect from all over Greece. He was included in the Seven Sages of Ancient Greece. By this time Lindos had become a great maritime trading city and had extended its trade zone to include Egypt, Cyprus and Syria. With the growing stature of the city, Kleoboulos improved the sanctuary to Athena by building a larger temple thought to have had a four columned portico at each end but without columns along the sides. The archaic staircase seen below the modern one may also be his contribution.

Shortly after the synoecism in 408 BC, when the three ancient cities on the island decided to combine and form a new city, Rhodes, the Lindians modernised their temple along more Classical lines. A large entrance gateway, a propylaeum, was added giving the temple more majesty and a new staircase was built over the archaic one effectively to isolate the temple from the rest of the acropolis.

Although Lindos lost some of its political importance after synoecism, its economic life was largely unaffected as was the fame of its sanctuary and it continued as a place of religious pilgrimage.

Around 342 BC the temple built by Kleoboulos burnt down together with the statue of Athena and many of the votive offerings. The Lindians promptly built a new one in its place repeating the original style and built an even bigger statue showing Athena standing and not seated as in the original. The statue this time was built with a body of gold plated wood and limbs of marble. One of the most interesting finds from Lindos, made in 1904, is the Temple Chronicle now housed in the museum in Copenhagen. This was written by a local scholar, Timachidas, in 99 BC and it describes many of the votive offerings of gold and silver by prominent historical figures of the day as well as some from mythical figures. One item on the list is the gift of a pair of bracelets from Helen of Troy. Other legends report that Helen of Troy gave a gold and silver vase made in the shape and form of her own breast by way of thanks since it was the sight of her breast

Opposite inset & below: *Lindos Acropolis*

that saved her from the wrath and revenge of Menelaus in Troy.

Later, in the Hellenistic Period around 200 BC, further developments took place on the acropolis which brought it to its final form. A huge double-winged covered colonnade, a stoa, was added on the north side embracing the steps up to the propylaeum and covering the whole width of the entrance. A small temple built in the north west corner is thought to be Roman. On the western outer flank of the acropolis is a fourth-century BC theatre cut into the rock with 27 rows of seats still preserved. Also outside the acropolis and near the theatre are the foundations of ancient walls believed to have formed part of a gymnasium.

The present fortifications are the work of the Knights of St John who, in the Byzantine era, remodelled and strengthened the walls of an earlier fortification.

Excavations were conducted by a Danish team under Klinch and Blinkenburg between 1902 and 1914. There have been many studies since including one by another Dane, Einar Dyggve, in 1952. It was Dyggve who produced a reconstruction model which is still widely quoted. The Italians in their period of occupation of the island undertook some restoration work which has not proved as durable as the original.

KEY TO MAP

1	Steps
2	Knight's Castle
3	Byzantine Church
4	Temple of Athena
5	Propylaia
6	Temple Forecourt
7	Doric Portico
8	Probale Roman Temple

a closing hour of 12 midnight is imposed on the music, although night clubs are allowed later hours. Persistent cries of pain from the wallets of the bar owners are usually sufficient to restore late hours, until the cycle starts again.

In antiquity, Lindos was believed to have had a population of around 16,000 compared to its present day 900. Before even the city of Rhodes was formed, Lindos was a powerful maritime trading post and it continued so into medieval times. The Knights of St John fortified the ancient acropolis to defend it against the troublesome Moslem forces. Lindos maintained its commercial power after the departure of the Knights by developing trading connections with Greece, Turkey and the Middle East. Buildings still remain from this sixthteenth-century period of prosperity. Wealthy sea captains built some of the grander stone houses, *archondika*, (see feature p.81) which were often typified by relief carvings of cable patterns around the doors and windows.

The way up to the acropolis follows the main road from the square past where the donkeys are stabled. In 1961 it was estimated that there were 6,583 donkeys on the island, now there are probably not even 83 and most of those are here at Lindos! Gone are the days when a little old lady in black riding a donkey was found round every corner. Most visitors will leave the island without seeing

excellent coffee, or up to roof garden restaurants. There is some good eating too in these smaller tavernas. Away from the main streets, the narrow side streets also a delight to wander where turning every corner brings some new surprise. There are some finely sculptured doorways where an open door may just allow a glimpse into some flower-decked pebbled courtyard. In the heart of the village, just off the main square lies the domed **Church of the Panagia**. This fifthteenth-church has a dark interior with a black and white pebbled floor and is decorated with eigtheenth-century frescos by Gregori of Symi. With typical polarisation, male saints are on the right and female on the left.

Lindos sleeps at night only out of the tourist season. Bars and discos keep the beat going just as long as trading laws will allow and this changes more often than the bus timetable. If the noise at night raises complaints on the island then

Opposite: *Artist capturing Lindos Acropolis scene*

one. But the donkeys are here to carry visitors up to the acropolis, at a price, of course. There is a choice and it is not too much trouble to make the ascent on your own feet. At least the donkeys are led on a longer and more gentle ascent and they do not mingle with the crowds. Going on foot, following the blue signs on the wall, takes you through the gauntlet of traders selling their wares and particularly the lace sellers who cover the embankment with their work on the final approach to the acropolis.

Lace making and embroidery has traditionally been centred on Lindos since Byzantine times. Tablecloths and mats are the chief items on display and in such numbers that it is easy to suspect that the whole enterprise is now on an organised commercial basis.

There is a charge to enter the acropolis. On Sunday during winter sites of antiquity and museums are free throughout Greece to encourage Greeks to visit and enjoy their own history.

Once through the entrance and before ascending the long flight of stairs (1), there is a relief carving in the grey rock face depicting the stern of a ship in remarkable detail. A bronze statue of Agesandros of Lindos, honoured for his virtue and care of the people, once stood on the largest part of the ship. At the top of the rather steep staircase (1), the castle is entered through a vaulted chamber (2) which formed part of the Governor's Palace; the ruins of this extend to the north wall of

the thirteenth-century Byzantine church of St John (3). The Sanctuary of Athena Lindia occupies much of the plateau. At the extreme south end of the site stands the temple dedicated to Athena (4) which had solid sides with four columns to the front and the rear. To the north of the temple lies the once impressive entrance halls, the propylaia (5) and the temple forecourt (6). These formed three sides of a large rectangle and were complete with rooms and colonnaded passages. Below this to the north is the huge double-winged stoa (7) of which there are still many columns standing although most are obscured by scaffolding from the ongoing restoration. Below the stoa is a large terrace supported by a series of vaults and still further north, according to dedications on some of the statue bases which are scattered around, lay the small Roman temple (8).

A view over the north wall gives an oversight of the large harbour which was once busy with ships of the great Lindian fleet. At the end of the promontory which encloses the large harbour lies the **tomb of Kleoboulos** which can be reached on

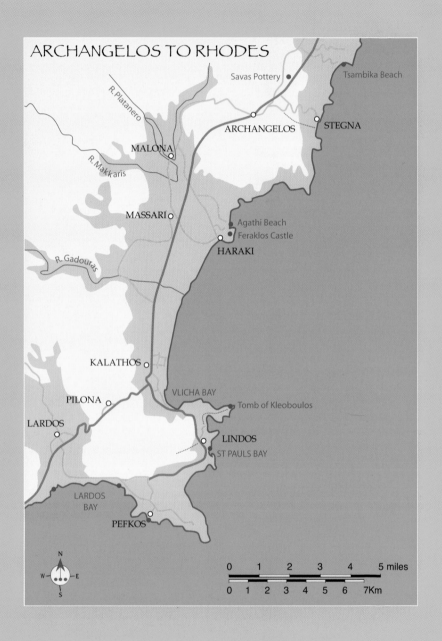

ARCHANGELOS TO RHODES

R. Platanero

Savas Pottery

Tsambika Beach

ARCHANGELOS

STEGNA

MALONA

R. Makkaris

MASSARI

Agathi Beach
Feraklos Castle

HARAKI

R. Gadouras

KALATHOS

VLICHA BAY

PILONA

Tomb of Kleoboulos

LARDOS

LINDOS

ST PAULS BAY

LARDOS
BAY

PEFKOS

N
W E
S

| 0 | 1 | 2 | 3 | 4 | 5 miles |
| 0 | 1 | 2 | 3 | 4 | 5 | 6 | 7Km |

Top: *View down onto the jetty from Lindos Acropolis*
Middle: *Scenes of Lindos beach*
Bottom: *Lindos bay*

foot (see feature box p.89). Assigning this burial tomb to Kleoboulos is apparently erroneous but the name still stands. Over the south wall the view is of the almost land locked bay where St Paul supposedly landed in AD58 and which is now named after him. It is known that St Paul did visit Rhodes on his way from Miletus to Syria to help convert the island to Christianity. Tucked away on the far side of St Paul's bay is the small chapel dedicated to him. Over to the west, looking almost straight down, the ancient theatre can be seen cut into the rock of the hillside. From here too the flat-topped village houses which cluster around the sides and the base of the acropolis can be surveyed. The greenery which squeezes between the houses is a reflection on the number of courtyards which are far less obvious when down amongst the houses.

With a good, deep stretch of fine sand, scenery second to none in the Aegean, an intimate feel in the enclosed bay and services immediately on hand, the beach at Lindos is an atmospheric place to be. Relaxing on a sun bed beneath a colourful umbrella, sipping a pina colada and gazing in awe at the curl of white sugar cubes around the acropolis hill is great if you can stand the heat. The sun works overtime in Lindos and swirls its light and heat around the amphitheatrical bowl with an energy which creates even more heat. It is easily the hottest spot on the island and in summer temperatures frequently get as high as 49°C (120°F). The smaller beach underneath the acropolis, connected by a walkway to the main beach, is well supplied with tavernas and just as popular.

It is easy to lose orientation walking through the narrow streets of the village which is the quickest way to get to **St Paul's Bay**. The only advice is to try and keep the acropolis to your left as you meander through the alleyways, although for much of the time the narrowness of the street blocks out the view. The route emerges by the flank of the acropolis near a car park. For a close view of the theatre just follow up the side of the car park until the fenced enclosure is reached. Entry is not permitted but the perimeter fence allows a fairly close approach. Continue down the lane to reach St Paul's Bay. This has a small shingle beach which is used for sunbathing but there are very limited facilities. The chapel to St Paul is tucked away under the rocks on the far side. This side of Lindos is as yet relatively undeveloped although new apartments in the traditional Lindian style are creeping ever closer to the bay.

On foot to the Tomb of Kleoboulos

Good footwear, like trainers, are advisable as there is some scrambling up the rocks near the start which requires a little agility. Allow around 1 hour 15 minutes for the return trip. Leave Lindos town by the main beach road and follow it down to the beach, keep going until the café at the far end is reached. Stay ahead through the café to locate steps cut into the rock behind. Climb these and follow a not too obvious path which leads upwards and to the right over the rocks. Once on top the path is more easily followed as it leads out towards the headland. (Alternatively, start the walk by forking left along the signposted track, off the first bend down the beach road.) A gulley holds up direct progress but once around this the way is clear to continue to the tomb. Looking over to the right, Lindos can be viewed from a different perspective.

The large circular monument where the footpath ends is the Hellenistic Tomb of Kleoboulos. Built around the first century BC, several centuries after the death of Kleoboulos, it was sturdily constructed from rectangular blocks and fitted with a conical roof. Inside, the burial chamber was rectangular and the grave in the rock floor. At some time in its history it was converted into the church of St Emilian.

Additional Information

Places to visit

Lindos Acropolis
Open: Every day 8am - 6.40pm but   only 12.30 -6.40pm on Monday.
Closed Monday out of season

T his tour looks at the southern part of the island, from Gennadi via Vati to Apolakia, to cross over to the west coast. Until a few years ago only the intrepid ventured beyond Lindos to explore the rural south and to discover the real Greek culture and people. All that is changing. Originally spurred on by the promise of a new international airport, developments have been taking place in villages like Pefkos and Gennadi and in coastal beauty spots where luxury hotels are springing into life. The airport remains a pipe dream but the hotels are reality. Holidaymakers gain a little and travellers lose a little. The old customs, the culture, learn to adapt to the steady invasion and to serve a new master. Backwaters still exist in villages like Asklipio where some of the old traditions continue as a way of life.

In this part of the south, the island is hilly rather than mountainous. It was, until 1987, richly cloaked in pine but no longer now are there dim forests where saprophytic orchids grew. In one of the island's worst natural disasters for years, fire ravaged virtually the whole of the south. Dead trees still scar the landscape. Left to its own devices, the cycle of nature plots its own certain course from destruction to regeneration. Taking advantage of the space and the light, broom has moved in to colonise the area and the hillsides now shine bright yellow throughout the spring. It will be future generations who see the forest eventually return. The whole area is very under populated, there are few villages and of these Lardos is by far the largest with a population of just 900.

Highlights along the route of this 60km (37.5 mile) journey include the resorts of Pefkos, Lardos as well as a number of villages, Asklipio, Gennadi, Apolakia including the nearby dam which is a good picnic spot, and Monolithos with its crusader castle.

Spectacular Lindos looks good from any angle. Taking the road out to the south gives yet another view which brings motorists to a halt for a last lingering look. Only from here is it easy to value the location of the old theatre cut into the rocky slope of the acropolis. The left turn for Pefkos is a mere 4km (2.5 miles) and there is a short descent into the village.

Pefkos (Pefka, Pefki) is more of a happening than anything planned which possibly adds to its charm. Perish the thought but Faliraki started as one street. There is one difference, the one street in Pefkos runs parallel to the coast and not towards it with the main beach down a narrow access road. The beach itself is good golden sand if on the narrow side while umbrellas and beds are on hand with tavernas not too far away. Accommodation is sprouting up in a higgledy-piggledy way, fully in character with the resort. The main street has most of the tavernas and shops in town which probably means it can be called the centre.

There is another beach to the west of the main beach which is a bit further away still, again with only a narrow access road. Fishermen's boats share this bay but beyond is a larger beach with access from the Lardos road. Pefkos is only a hop, skip and jump away from Lindos yet in might be a million miles.

Leave Pefkos by the coastal road to rejoin shortly the road from Lindos. **Lardos bay** looms on the left; another area enjoying a boom in tourist development. **Lardos** village lies across the main coast road shortly reached. Head for the main square for signs of life and the cafés. Apart from the comings and goings of ordinary folk and a bit of shop gazing, there is little to keep you away from the beach.

Back on the coastal road heading south, there is a glimpse of Lardos beach with its umbrellas and tavernas. It is a 10km (6.25 mile) run down to the Asklipio turn off but tiny **Glystra beach** snuggling into a crescent shaped cove is almost too inviting to pass without a closer look. Expectations of an invasion of unadulterated expansive Rhodian landscapes are dashed immediately around the short inland loop. Here high class Hotel Rodos Maris fills both sides of the road. With more imagination than usual, the architect has borrowed a little something from the past and introduced columns and porticoes to the neo-classical to create an impression of a village evolved from antiquity. Almost next to it is another four star hotel, the Rodos Princess.

Turn right at the junction signposted Asklipio, head up into the village and park in the car park by the church.

Asklipio, watched over by a medieval castle, sprawls down the hillside without the benefit of a grand design but all the better for that. A traditional village in all senses it takes its name from Asklepius, the Greek god of medicine and Apollo's favourite son. There is the story of tragic love mixed up here which ended up with the raven, previously white, being turned black. Apollo's lover Koronis whilst pregnant with Asclepius took another lover, a mere mortal. This news was carried to Apollo by a raven who was promptly turned black for her trouble. Still in something of a mood, Apollo killed Koronis and committed her body to the pyre but drew the child from her just before the flames struck. Asklepius later went off to learn medicine from Chiron, the centaur. The village here was once was the island's

Opposite page: Dormition of the Blessed Virgin, Asklipio

healing centre with a hospital and doctors. Even now the sick still come but to seek healing at the church.

Like most small villages, it is alive in the morning with locals going about their daily routines. In the afternoon everybody sleeps. Siesta time is an undying tradition in Greece, summer or winter, and little moves between 2 and 5pm. Outside ovens are seen in many villages but here they are still regularly used. Blackened fronts and stored wood are the give-away signs but to see the bread makers in action, featured on p.94, take your chance morning or evening.

The village here is no stranger to tourism, but most of it, until recently, Greek tourism drawn by the Byzantine church **the Dormition of the Blessed Virgin**, found at the entrance to the village. Built in AD1060, it started as a cross but extended later to accommodate a larger congregation. There are some fine frescos to see in the church for which, unusually, there is a small entry charge. Just next to the church is a recently opened **museum** displaying ancient religious artefacts, old bibles and ikons in the one room whilst the second room depicts the old way of village life with agricultural tools, bread making implements and even an old olive oil press. This is a co-operative venture by the villagers themselves who contributed many of the exhibits and well worth a few moments.

Many of the houses in this village, as on the whole island, are simple flat-roofed cubic structures without any redeeming architectural features. Inside is quite another matter. A number of the houses here are of the traditional Rhodian village style, as described on p.96. The easiest way to see one is to find Sylvia's café which is

Traditional Village Bread Making

Using the outside ovens for making bread is still practised by the old people of Asklipio and a number of other villages on the island. Bread is made just once a week in sufficient quantity to last the family until the next bake the following week. The ovens are pressed into more frequent use only on festive occasions and particularly at Easter time when vast quantities of *koulourakia lambriatika*, Easter biscuits, are made.

Typically, these outdoor ovens are fired up the previous evening using mostly pine wood and allowed to burn all night. There is no vent so the initial flames and the smoke issue out of the front opening which is eventually closed with a simple metal shutter. Overnight the fire burns to red embers heating the stone floor and the walls very thoroughly.

Mixing the ingredients also starts the evening before allowing the dough to rise overnight. The shaped loaf, usually round, is stamped on top with a personal mark if the oven is shared with other users. The stamp is a wood carved roundel which may be hand made although commercial ones are available and sometimes seen in the older shops or in village hardware stores. Carefully wrapped in a tablecloth, placed on a board and covered again, the loaves are carried to the outside oven for baking.

Preparing the oven to receive the loaves is an important first step. Pushing the glowing embers to one side, the centre of the oven is thoroughly cleaned using a simple broom especially prepared on each occasion. Twigs of the evergreen mastic tree, *Pistacio lentiscus*, are tied to a wooden stave to make the broom. The mastic tree is one which has been used for centuries by the Greeks for medicinal reasons but chiefly for the fragrant gummy resin it yields. It is still grown commercially on the island of Chios where the gum is used in chewing gum, valued for preserving the gums and sweetening the breath, to flavour sweets, to make incense and, not least, in the manufacture of resins. Mastic is chosen for this use, not just because it is effective in brushing away the dust, but also for the clean fragrance it imparts which is believed to have antiseptic properties.

The loaves are transferred to the oven on a wooden spade and placed directly on the oven floor. When baking gets underway, the top of each loaf is brushed with water to give a good glaze. Another broom is used for this, one made from fresh sage twigs tied to a long stave, again to impart flavour. Any small piece of dough left over is usually made up into a small loaf which goes in the oven last and comes out first. Sometimes, a child or a tourist passing at the right moment might just receive the gift of a small loaf with the customary warning delivered by all mothers that eating hot bread makes you ill. A small sprig of fresh sage pushed through the bread allows the lucky recipient to carry away the hot loaf, and it tasted really good!

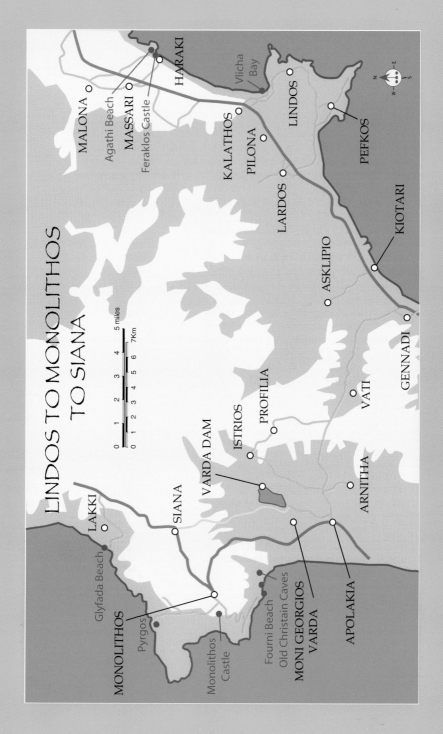

Traditional Homes

The traditional village folk houses, seen in Asklipio, Archangelos and Koskinou and many of the older villages on Rhodes, have only a single space inside. This simple style of house, seen also in other Dodecanese islands, has its roots in the era of the Knights of St John or more particularly in inheritance rights from that period. Here the first born daughter inherited the house and all her mother's possessions while the other children were expected to move out. Furthermore, it was a father's duty to provide a house for each of his daughters as a dowry. This basic, simple structure, intended to house a complete family, parents and children, provided the most economical solution.

Apart from the doorway, there may be no other opening or perhaps a window in the front wall. Inside, a wide archway indicates a division between the living section and the sleeping quarters with the floor usually set with black and white pebbles. Peripheral benches and raised platforms provided the furnishing leaving the central area clear. The fireplace occupied a corner by the front door. The matrimonial bed was a raised platform about 1.5m (4ft 9in) high which was enclosed by an embroidered curtain, a *sperveri*, The children also slept on a platform, normally slightly lower, either close by or on the opposite wall. By the fireplace was the *soufas*, a low platform upholstered with carpets or mattresses for sitting and dining. *Soufas*, like the English word sofa, probably derived from the Arabic *suffah*. Storage cupboards for bedding and linen and for oil, wine and food were arranged under the high platforms. Benches completed the furnishing which also served for storage.

Embroideries, fabrics, plates and pitchers were all used as interior decoration, especially plates. Decorative plates were especially important and would cover the whole side of the wall facing the door relieved only by a mirror. Often the plates were sent home by migrant family and a vast number indicated a form of wealth.

located by walking ahead from the church car park through the next open space then bearing left. Sylvia is Greek Australian with good English and is happy to talk about life in the village. She has refurbished the interior of the house next to her café in the traditional style and is happy to show interested visitors inside.

Above Asklipio broods the ruins of a medieval **Crusader castle**. It is a 15 minute walk to reach it following the broad track which starts just to the right of the toilets. After an impressive entrance, there is little to see inside the castle except for good views over the countryside but care needs to be taken for uncovered wells. As the story goes, there was at one time a tunnel from one of the houses to the castle so that villagers could secretly gain refuge from raiding pirates.

Leave Asklipio back to the coast road and cross directly over to reach the beach and the area known as **Kiotari**. This was the site of the original village of Asklipio but it was forced inland by piracy probably in the period from the seventh to the ninth century. Piracy at this time was particularly troublesome to the islanders and many old settlements were destroyed or driven inland. Fortifications too were built and it is from this time that the castle at Asklipio may have its origins.

The land by the coast here belongs to the church and the villagers are allowed to build simple beach huts which they use in summer. A section of the old national road runs both north and south along the coast. Moles and sand-spits divide up the shoreline into smaller bays, some sandy, others strewn with seaweed looking like wood shavings. Shaded by tamarisk trees and lapped by an ever-blue sea, it contrives to be picturesque in a way not seen elsewhere on Rhodes.

Running southwards, Kiotari beach blends seamlessly with Gennadi's beach. Return to the main coastal route to continue south. Ignore the turn off right to Apolakia which will be the onward route shortly but first take a look at the coast by turning next left. A colourful rash of sun shades in orderly rank is as unexpected as rain in August this far down south but this shingle beach is the playground of fast growing **Gennadi**. Located inland of the main road, Gennadi has seen steady tourist development over the past few years outgrowing its tag of 'sleepy hamlet'. Wander at will and try to find the Italian built police station but without a recognisable centre it is hard to know where to start and finish. Not so difficult to find are modern supermarkets and tavernas which are scattered around but the place only really comes to life at night when people return from the beach.

Leave Gennadi by taking the road out to **Apolakia**. Flashes of electric blue skimming around the fields here are likely to be bee-eaters, especially if their soft liquid chrrup call is also heard. They tend to congregate on the telephone wires along the roadside so keep the binoculars handy. Apiary is common in the south, but the

Pyrgos on Foot

There is nothing at Pyrgos except the pyrgos, a watch tower, and a long since deserted settlement. Problems in the defence of the long stretch of hostile coastline north from here were solved by castles at Monolithos and Kritinia with a chain of watch towers between. The tower at Pyrgos is particularly well preserved and this walk provides one of the very few opportunities for a close look. There is another one to see at Glyfada Beach, but not in such good condition, for those who follow the side trip described in the following chapter.

This walk takes place over tracks which are generally comfortable underfoot but stout shoes or trainers are strongly recommended. It is downhill all the way and uphill on the return. The distance is 12km (7.5 miles) for the round trip and it requires about 4 hours walking time in addition to time spent at the site which makes a full half day excursion. To find the start of the walk, drive out of Monolithos on the castle road and look for the track on the right, in just over 1km (0.6miles). It is identified by a sign for Kimisala and a battered no entry road sign. Park here and set off on foot down this track which leads at first along a contour of Mount Akramitis on the seaward side. There are fairly open views in the early part of the walk. Stay left in just over half an hour, where the main track forks around to the right, and descend into the shade of the pine trees. Eventually, after a steady descent ignoring tracks off left, when the sea more or less comes into view, the way divides. To the left leads to the tower on the coast while to the right is the remains of an old settlement. The path down to the pyrgos provides a good overview of the old settlement. Return by the same route.

Early Christian caves at Fourni

Apolakia

Above & below: Monolithos castle

beekeepers can hardly be pleased to be supporting such a good population of bee-eaters. The surrounding low, rolling, scrub covered hills, lively and colourful in spring retire drab and listless in summer, but scent the air with heady aromatic odours of rosemary and thyme.

On entering Apolakia, watch out for the road off right signposted 'Dam'. It is a 4km (2.5 mile) diversion along a surfaced road to reach a viewpoint over the artificial lake of Varda Dam. Normally very peaceful, it is an ideal place to picnic and unwind from driving. Even this lake assumes the Aegean blue of the sea and beyond, on a distant hillside, the white houses of Siana cluster below the peak. The road continues from the dam as a track all the way up to Siana. For those with itchy feet, it is around 14km (8.75 miles) for the return walk. To the side of the dam lies the little white church of **Ag. Theotokou**.

Apolakia exists around a major junction and is a great watering hole. It only seems to come to life with the arrival of the daily bus. The wise elders drink coffee in the kafeneon whilst everybody else is out in the field busy growing melons. It is very much an agricultural town which sees only a passing tourist trade. Once through, turn north for the 11km (6.9 mile) run to Monolithos. It is a gradual rise towards the Akramitis mountains along a meandering route through forested countryside. On the eastern side of the island, the rolling hills descend gently towards the coast leaving some coastal plain. Here on the west coast, more particularly from Monolithos northwards to Skala Kamiros, the mountain crowds in on the sea and the road is often forced to a higher level.

Monolithos village slumbers at the foot of Akramitis and is little disturbed even when the coaches thunder through en route to **Monolithos castle**. And the castle is firmly on the tourist agenda. The road runs alongside the village so, unless an effort is made to get out and walk around, little is seen of the way of life there. Most of the tavernas too are located on the through route to catch the passing trade, especially coach parties. The road down to the castle is good but drive slowly so the view point from above is not missed. Monolithos castle sits astride Monopetra, a blunted needle of grey rock rising precipitously to 236m (775ft). No fairy tale castle this, but a real life impregnable fortress built by the Grand Master d'Aubusson. The thick walls thread around the top and inside is the white church of **Ag. Panteleimon**. Steps lead up from the car park below the castle to an area enclosed by the walls. From the top the views are absorbing both along the coastline and of the offshore islands including Halki.

Following the coast road for 4km (2.5 miles) after leaving the castle leads down to **Fourni**. There is a small beach of sandy shingle at Fourni with sun beds and a canteen in high season. It is not the beach but the early Christian caves which provide the interest here. To reach them, cross the beach heading for the base of the spit of cream-

Souma and Ouzo

Wine has a by-product in the form of grape skins, seeds, pulp and stems, known collectively as raki, which can be distilled to produce a strong spirit. Subtle flavours are introduced by the infusion of certain herbs, like fennel or aniseed, before distillation and all these products were originally called raki. Ouzo has grown out of this process. No longer is it made from the wine residues but from pure alcohol made from molasses with the addition of aniseed and other herbs. Well made ouzo contains around 46% alcohol and is usually taken with ice or water. Dilution with water liberates the aromatic oil anethole, introduced from the aniseed, to turn the drink milky, sometimes more so or less so depending on the actual manufacture. Generally, dense cloudiness indicates high quality. To the casual drinker, all ouzos taste much the same but the various brand names have different followings, some achieving wider recognition throughout the country than others. For the Greeks, ouzo is more than just a drink, it is blue sky, warm air, sunshine and even more, it is the breath of the soul, a drink to share for male bonding. Traditionally, it must be taken with a little food, with nuts or mezedes. Mezedes is a small plate of food, typically a few small bite size pieces of bread, some olives, a bit of cheese, a meat ball or anything that the taverna is cooking that day. Now it is usually a few nuts but in some of the older villages ouzo is still served with mezedes.

Souma is the product of distillation of the wine residues, or the alcohol from small, reject grapes. It is made almost everywhere that wine is made although it has different names on different islands and in different parts of the country. Here on Rhodes it is souma; on the mainland, particularly the north, it is tsipouro; on Crete it is called tsikoudia. Much of it is made illegally but here in Siana some farmers were granted a licence by the Italians which was never rescinded and is still recognised by the present authorities. In most places it is not possible to buy souma to sample or take away because it is usually illegally made but here in Siana you can do both of these.

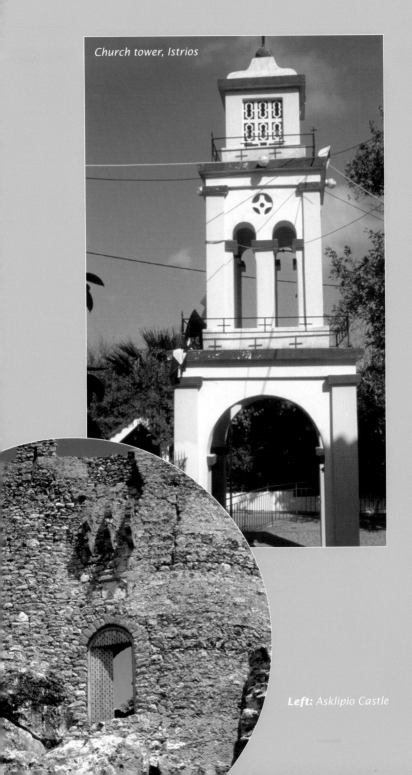

Church tower, Istrios

Left: Asklipio Castle

Siana Church

coloured rock at the far end. Follow the narrow path to wind up and round onto the top of this. The caves are well concealed on the southern face and there are steps which lead down to them, although they are not especially easy to locate. Be warned, these old, badly worn steps are close to the edge and dangerous. Despite this, people still go down! The caves date back as far as the seventh century when Christians went into hiding to escape persecution from first the Persians and then the Arabs.

Return back along the same road towards the castle then the town of Monolithos and continue northwards to **Siana**. Wending through pine alongside Akramitis, the scenery takes on a mountainous aspect with glimpses of the stark, barren summit of Ataviros, the highest peak on the island. Siana arrives quickly enough and there is usually space to park near the church. Like a number of hinterland villages on Rhodes, it is built on a hillside and is best seen on foot. Looking south, the dam visited in the earlier part of this tour can be clearly seen. Siana is famous for its honey and its souma. Four kinds of honey are made, according to the season: flower honey from the pollen of spring flowers is made in April and May, thyme honey in June and July, pine honey in September and October and heather honey in December. Souma is a strong spirit made illegally in other parts of the island but, by a quirk of history, is legally made under licence here by just one supplier. Details of its manufacture are featured on p.101. Anyone looking to try a sample of this local firewater can buy it from numerous roadside traders. Most sell unlabelled bottles of souma believing this sidesteps the law.

Below & opposite: *Honey for sale, Siana*

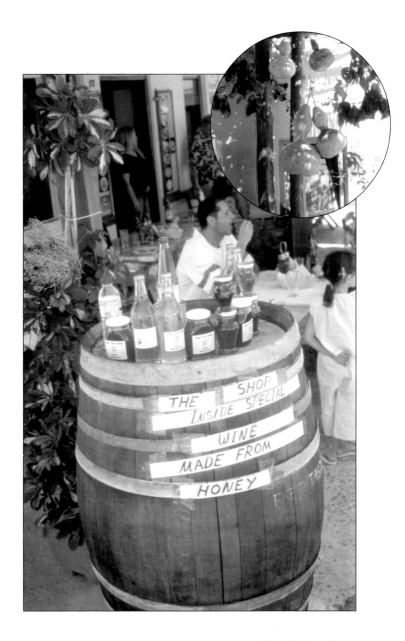

THE SHOP
INSIDE SPECIAL
WINE
MADE FROM
HONEY

Throughout history the western coast below Kamiros has never attracted settlements of any great size or number. Poor access to the sea, a hostile physical geography, poor land quality for agriculture or livestock and even unsuitable climatic factors are all deterrents. With a fairly constant westerly wind, and some altitude above the sea, this region is distinctly cooler in summer and probably cold in winter. It is this cooler micro climate as well as edaphic factors which now support the island's most successful region of viniculture centred near Embonas. Piracy too remained a problem, especially from the seventh to the ninth centuries, and where tempting cultivable land lay on the slopes in view of the sea, temporary summer farm settlements developed. Lakki, visited shortly is one such settlement which still farms in the same way even today. Defending the coastline too was problematic but solved by having castles at Monolithos and Kritinia and a chain of watch towers, pyrgoi, on the coastal areas between. One of these near Monolithos is featured in a walk, see p.98 and another on the side trip down to Glyfada Beach described shortly. In the time of the Knights of St John, these towers were constantly manned and in times of danger signalled by either primitive semaphore or pigeon by day and beacon fires by night to ensure that the alarm was passed from fortress to fortress.

North of Kamiros, the mountains progressively fall away and the amount of cultivable land increases as does the number of settlements. Closer still to Rhodes town, especially from the airport northwards, is some of the densest development on the island and much of it for tourism. Why this area in particular has seen such development is hard to appreciate. Certainly it is convenient for both Rhodes town and the airport but the beaches, mostly narrow, usually shingle and sometimes non-existent, in no way match those of the east coast. It is a very windy part of the island too although this comes as something of a blessing in the heat of high summer. Almost as a compensation, the accommodation offered in this area is amongst the finest on the island and it has a near monopoly of luxury class hotels. The Rodian Amathus Beach Hotel, for example, offers bags of facilities including an indoor and three outdoor swimming pools, besides a section of private beach with subway access. There are bars, satellite television, shops and the excellent **Amathusia Spa**, again open to the general public. Where the spa is concerned, it is a case of being spoilt for choice as the extensive range of treatments and therapies are well worth sampling. Also open to the general public is the award winning Greek Taverna, Varkarola, providing a high class cuisine. Fish food addicts will not wish to miss the Lobster evening and the in-house chocolate soufflé is a taste bud delight. The hotel also boasts conference and banqueting facilities, ideal for large meetings or gatherings of special interest groups.

Wild and rugged scenery in the early part of this tour gives way to coastal plains and cultivation but there are plenty of highlights along the way; Kritinia and its castle, the ancient city of Kamiros, another ancient site, Filerimos, and the resort areas of Trianda and Ixia.

Fortresses & Castles on Rhodes

As a result of intense pirate activity in the seventh to ninth centuries AD and the activities of the Knights of St John, the island has a remarkable number of castles and fortresses of which many have survived. The seven principal ones are at Rhodes town, Archangelos, Feraklos, Lindos, Asklipio, Monolithos and Kritinia all of which are visited in the appropriate chapter.

Defence against the infidel Moslems was an ongoing concern of the Knights which spurred them into almost constant building and reinforcing. Twelve fortresses were known to exist under Grand Master E.B. Degli Orsini in 1479 which had to serve 44 settlements but the full total was thought to be around 16. Each settlement was instructed on evacuation procedures and assigned to the various castles. Settlements at Gennadi, Kalathos and Lardos were assigned to Lindos castle for example. Other castles mentioned in these instructions were located at Apolakia, Lahania, Katavia, Apollonia, Salakos, Fanes and Villanova as well as the fortifications at Filerimos. In addition to these, there are castle remains found at Lardos and Mesanagros. Towers, *pyrgoi*, were also built around coastal regions, especially on the west coast as an integral part of the elaborate defences. Some of these are still in good condition, especially the one at Pyrgos which is visited on foot in chapter 4.

Monday is not a good day to see the ancient cities when both are closed.

Leaving Siana northwards, the road continues at high level with the stark grey mass of Mount Ataviros exerting an even greater presence on the right. By contrast, the offshore islands over left of Alimnia, Tragoussa, Strongili and Makri have an ethereal quality, floating in a blueness of uncertainty where sea and sky merge to banish the horizon. Scene gazing or not, once beyond the Ag. Isidoros road, watch out for the left turn down to **Glyfada Beach**. Despite its name, it has no beach. If lunch calls, it is worth the round trip of 12km (7.5 miles) to a choice of two tavernas, one of them right on the shoreline. With no passing traffic they are really atmospheric places to eat. Part way down is a view of Lakki, partly deserted but still used as it always has been for summer farming. Captain Gregoris' fish taverna is first encountered but follow right along the seashore to reach Paradise fish taverna. Next to this are the remains of an old watch tower, a *pyrgos*.

Most of the roads leading off the main road in this section seem to arrive with minimum announcement and are easy to miss. This is true of the left fork leading into **Kritinia**. The modern road detours quite circuitously around the village with a link road from either end. Take the narrow left fork down through the village and park where you can, perhaps past the main church. Here is a village which, although on a slope, for once does not straggle down the hillside. Not too far from the sea, the location is, nevertheless, hidden but within sight of the castle. Thought to be settled by immigrants from Crete (Kriti), Kritinia has something almost unique on the island but common elsewhere in Greece, a true village square, a platea. This is located below the church giving commanding views down towards the castle. Two tavernas compete for custom but whichever, with plenty of colour from the surrounding floral display, it is a relaxing atmosphere to sit and watch the world go by. The village has a small **folk museum** but this is located in the imposing building outside the village on the main road heading north. Local costumes and farming implements are amongst the exhibits as too is a tripod cradle which held baby whilst mother worked the land and hollow gourds used not just to carry water but also to keep it cool. Only small but well worth a stop. The panoramic views from the café terrace here are very persuasive.

In sight from here, **Kritinia castle** is the next port of call so watch for the narrow road off left signposted for the castle. Just before the entrance to the castle, one of the local ladies usually leaps out with a notice which explains that she is in charge of the castle and solely responsible for its upkeep and maintenance. While there is no charge for entrance, the notice explains, it would help if some of her fruit or vegetables were purchased! To lend authority to this, her Greek identity card is usually proffered. This amusing local enterprise usually works

Castle Circular on Foot

Below, but out of sight of the castle, a gorge cuts through the hills to the sea. From the coastal end of this gorge, a fairly short but uphill footpath returns to the castle completing an attractive circular walk. The complete walk takes around 1 hour 30 minutes and, while some of it is over tracks, much is over stony footpaths which for comfort and safety demand good footwear.

Follow the track down from the castle entrance and turn right at the first junction. Keep ahead to cross tracks and turn left. Stay along this track as it describes a U, with the castle over left, before swinging right. Keep ahead briefly on meeting a tarmac road but almost immediately fork right onto a track. Follow this track towards the sea, ignoring two tracks off left, as it gradually descends to the valley bottom. Just before reaching the streambed in the bottom, fork right onto a clear path which rises a little and heads off around the hillside. The deep ravine falls away on the left but the path stays at a high level for a time giving spectacular views then descends gradually to the seashore. Stay close to the right hillside alongside the wire fence to reach the shore where there is a partially excavated ancient site. Look for the path from the shore here that ascends the hill back more directly towards the castle. This well defined path leads in winding ascent to emerge up against another wire fence blocking the original route. Stay left uphill to reach a fairly open area on top. Continue, with the sea on the left, towards what turns out to be the metal bars of a tennis court. Make for the right of the court and end of a track. Unwind the temporary fencing down the side of the court to access the track. This minor track leads to a track from a white house down to the right. Turn left towards the castle. Ignore the first track left but take the second left to return to the castle and complete the circuit.

Below Kritinia castle

Above & below: *Kritinia castle*

because the produce looks so fresh and there may be more than one of these entrepreneurs. Still, it is a long time since the castle has been swept out.

Perched on a rock (130m/430ft), it is not too much of a climb to enter the castle. This is another built by the Knights of St John originally on three levels with each level assigned to a different Grand Master. Apart from remnants of the chapel, there is little to see of internal structures but there are some excellent coastal views and it is interesting to wander around.

Return northwards from the castle to the main road. Almost immediately on rejoining the main road, be prepared to turn left into **Kamiros Skala** which is nothing more than a small harbour and a handful of tavernas. This was the port of ancient Kamiros but possibly too far away to have developed significantly.

The boat to and from Halki docks here, arriving from Halki in the morning and returning at 2.30pm Monday to Saturday. A bus from Rhodes town serves both the arriving and departing boats. To spend a day on Halki midweek requires a two night stopover, unless a few hours is enough with one night there and a 6.00am return. Sunday is different. A day trip runs Sunday departing Kamiros Skala 9.00am promptly and Halki at 5.00pm. At the moment there are no buses on a Sunday from Rhodes town. See Chapter 10 for further details on Halki.

Kamiros Skala is the place for fresh fish and the tavernas are popular with the islanders, especially at weekends. Unfortunately, the tour parties know it too so lunchtimes can get crowded. Apart from the coach parties, it is a fairly sleepy place unless a fish catch is being landed or the Halki boat is around.

With the mountains left behind and down again at sea level, agriculture takes over with a sea of plastic greenhouses. It is worth diverting into **Mandriko** to see its impressive church. The peaceful ambience of the taverna next to the church is a welcome oasis for a quiet lunch or drink. Continuing north, picturesque seascapes come and go as the road follows the coastline towards ancient Kamiros. Turn right for the short diversion to the ancient city and park in the area outside the gates.

Kamiros was one of the three ancient cities on the island. First settled by the Mycenaeans, it was later colonised by Dorians around 1100BC. It grew steadily in prosperity keeping apace with the other Dorian cities of Ialysos and Lindos but only until the synoecism of 408BC leading to the formation of a new city, Rhodes. Kamiros went into decline but continued to be inhabited into the early centuries of Christianity until, at some time around this period, it was finally abandoned. The hills surrounding the ancient city are full of cemeteries which have proved of enormous interest to the archaeologists and yielded many fine pieces now housed in the museum in Rhodes town, including the grave stele of Kroto and Tamarista.

The old city was built on a hollow slope of a hillside facing

Opposite: Ancient Kamiros

northwards. The residential part of the town occupied the lower slopes whilst the acropolis, including the religious and public buildings, sat on the top of the hill behind. Unlike the other two cities, Ialysos and Lindos, it was not fortified. After centuries in oblivion, it was rediscovered in 1859 and excavated by Biliotti and Salzman and further excavated by the Italians from 1929 onwards. Revealed now is a ground plan of houses, streets and sanctuaries covering an extensive area and representing the finest example in Greece of the residential sector of an ancient city.

The entrance leads into a sanctuary with a fountain. To the north of this, and first encountered, lie the remains of a Doric temple of unknown dedication. Further east is the Sanctuary of the Altars which was a sacrificial area with nine alters, including a large one, and all still in good condition. Running uphill to the south is the main street which gives a close view of the remains of the domestic dwellings. On the left, higher up, are the remains of a private house with part of the colonnade restored. Parts of the sophisticated drainage system are visible at the top of the street.

On the highest point is a sixth-century BC cistern and behind, a huge third-century BC stoa fully 200m (660yds) long with two rows of Doric columns. There were rooms behind the columns which were probably hotel rooms for worshippers visiting the temple. The temple of Athena Kamiros lay behind and only parts of the foundations now remain. From the stoa there is an excellent overview of the old city.

Retrace the route down to the coast road to continue northwards. If refreshments are in order, or if it is time for a meal, Old and New Kamiros tavernas await on the coast below the site. They offer

Ialysos through the ages

Known as Filerimos since the middle ages, previously called Ialysos and referred to by the ancients as Archaia, even the name causes confusion but it does hold clues to its origins.

According to legend and to votive offerings found during excavations, this fertile area was first occupied by the Phoenicians from a very early period. Later, around 1500 BC, the Minoans arrived from Crete to set up trading posts and they too chose Ialysos only to be superseded a century later by the Mycenaean Archaeans. It was the style of Mycenaeans to build strong fortresses, usually on a hill, to guard an area of fertile land and the plateau on Mt Filerimos was the ideal place. Many centuries later, long after the Mycenaeans had fallen to the Dorian invaders around the twelve century BC, the memory was kept alive by the use of the name Archaia for the acropolis of Ialysos.

Remains of Mycenaean settlements have been found around Trianda and a large number of tombs from the same period have been discovered on the surrounding low hills.

The Dorians, who spoke a form of Greek, were invaders from the north who swept down into Greece and spread to the islands. A regression followed their arrival in which material wealth declined, the art of writing was lost, no building of significance took place and the population shrank. When Greece grew out of this dark age and progressed again, Ialysos, like Kamiros and Lindos, started to flourish and did so until 408BC when the three cities agreed to combine and build a new city, Rhodes. Its history did not finish there. A large temple to Athena Polias and Zeus Polieus was built on the acropolis around the third or second century BC and this, it is believed, was built on the site of an earlier temple. Even earlier was the Doric fountain, uncovered by a landslip in 1926, built around the fourth century BC.

An early fifth or sixth century AD Christian basilica obliterated part of the old temple and hastened its destruction. Later the ancient acropolis was used for military purposes first by the Byzantines when they were besieged by the Genoans in 1248 and then by the Knights. It was their first stronghold when they arrive on the island in 1306. The Knights improved the fortifications and built a monastery and a church on the site of the old basilica. The present day monastery with its courtyard and cells was restored by the Italians.

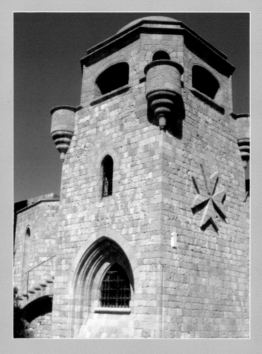

Above & below left: Church of our Lady, Filerimos
Below right: Filerimos

sunbeds and umbrellas on the shore to entice customers to linger but, for a more rustic experience, continue further north. Akroyiali taverna, just before Kalavarda, enjoys a delightful ambience. It looks on to a quiet stretch of beach where the fishermen, if not landing a catch, are kept busy sorting out their nets.

It seems reasonable to expect that the coast road is the major route so to give way at the Kalavarda junction comes as a surprise. Tourism is slowly creeping down this coast although it almost seems without reason. **Theologos** (Tholos), off the road to the right, has a surprising number of tourist rooms. The remains of a temple to Apollo, theatre and excavations of what was once a fairly significant complex lie just inland. To visit, follow signs by turning sharp back right round the petrol station. The theatre lies behind excavations on the left of the road and the remains of the **Temple to Apollo** on the right, before reaching the village.

Traffic density increases when **Paradissi** and the airport is reached. Although Paradissi is virtually on the runway, it does have rooms and tavernas which makes it useful for visitors arriving late or departing very early. From here the building density alongside the road increases steadily, particularly noticeable from Kremasti onwards. **Kremasti** is one of the larger villages on the island which has remained Greek and managed to integrate tourism without being overtly touristic. It has hotels and rooms and offers a pebbly beach with the attendant sun parasols and beds. Life stirs on

August 14/15th with a panayiria, a **festival for the Assumption of the Virgin Mary** with street fairs and a market. In contrast, **Trianda** a little nearer to Rhodes town has a much heavier and more obvious involvement in tourism and, with over 7,000 inhabitants, is the most populous village on the island outside Rhodes town. It is also known as Ialysos after the ancient city and both names are in common use. The remains of the ancient city itself up on the hill inland are now known by the modern name of Filerimos.

Heading towards Rhodes town it is more convenient to look at the coastal area of Trianda first before heading up to Filerimos. A one way system operates which allows a left at the widely spaced set of lights which then leads down past tourist shops and tavernas to the sea front. If a good beach is a high priority then the narrow stretch of sand and shingle will disappoint but, nevertheless, it is well decked with sun umbrellas angled against the constant breeze which is meat to the windsurfers. Looking northwards, there are views along the coast to Rhodes town. Hotels are located in areas both on the seaward side and the inland side of the main through road and the village is well connected by bus to Rhodes.

For **Filerimos**, follow the one way system back to the main road and continue across at the traffic lights. Open countryside is not far away which is appreciated as the road winds and twists up the pine clad slopes of Mt Filerimos occasionally presenting arresting views. There is plenty of space so parking is no problem .

The summit plateau, 267m (876ft) was the home of the acropolis of the ancient city of **Ialysos**, one of the three ancient cities of the island. The city itself spread over the north western slopes towards the village of Kremasti but now interest centres only on the summit plateau.

From the entrance, a stepped avenue shaded by cypress leads up to the rebuilt **Church of Our Lady of Filerimos** and the monastery. The church has four chapels, the outer of which was built by Grand Master d'Aubusson and the innermost still has the floor of the original early Christian church with the mosaic fish decoration. Solitude reigns in the cloister at the rear of the church where the monks' cells are each marked with a mosaic plaque, each showing a different apostle. The remains in front of the church are those of the **Temple of Athena Polias and Zeus Polieus**. This temple was a larger version of the one at Lindos with a vestibule entrance guarded by four columns and an enclosed section at the rear, also with four columns. The remains of a paved floor of an even older Phoenician temple can be seen in front of one of the rectangular statue bases.

In front of the temple to Athena is the small underground Byzantine chapel of **Agios Georgios**. whose walls were decorated with frescos by the Knights of St John around the 14th to 15th century.

Returning down the stepped

Below: *Beach at Trianda, keeping the breeze at bay*

Ancient Kamiros

SIANA BACK TO RHODES TOWN

ANCIENT KAMIROS

ENTRANCE

MAIN STREET

HOUSES

	KEY TO MAP		
1	Sanctuary	8	Hellenistic Houses
2	Exedra	9	Stoa
3	Doric Temple	10	Sixth-Century BC Cistern
4	Doorway	11	Pits
5	Retaining Wall	12	Temple to Athena
6	Steps	13	Public Baths
7	Sacrifical Area	14	Ancient Wall

N
W — E
S

FANES
SORONI
KALAVARDA
THEOLOGOS (THOLOS)
PARADISSI
International Airport
KRESMASTI
TRIANDA
RHODES TOWN
KRITIKA
Airstrip
Mount Filerimos
TRIS
IXIA
FILERIMOS (IALYSOS)

avenue, a left turn at the bottom leads to the remains of the **Doric fountain** which was luckily revealed after a landslip in 1926. (This is not always open to access.) It was a highly ornamental roofed fountain built around the fourth century BC with a facade of Doric columns. The water reached the fountain by a channel cut in the rock behind and was delivered through two of the four lions' heads, the other two were ornamental. There were more lions' heads at the front of the basin. A now illegible inscription on one of the posts laid down the law about the use of the fountain.

Back at the base of the stepped avenue, the way opposite the steps is a road called Calvary (Golgotha) lined by fourteen copper reliefs representing the Stations of the Cross erected by the Italians. It leads to a huge cross and platform viewpoint looking over the western side of the island. Absorbing views include the two airports, Trianda, Kremasti, and Maritsa whilst looking to the distance, the two highest points on the island, the wooded slopes of Profitis Ilias and the barren summit of Ataviros, can both be picked out.

Available at the on-site café/shop is a speciality of Filerimos, the seven herb liqueur.

Heading northwards again towards Rhodes town, Trianda merges seamlessly with Ixia, the appearance of giant hotels announcing the change. Here are most of the luxury class hotels on the island, the Rodian Amathus Beach Hotel, Hilton, Rodos Palace Hotel, Olympic Palace and Hotel Cosmopolitan all lie in this area. The list seems endless but with a busy main road outside the door and a small, often crowded, beach beyond, all attempt and most succeed in making their hotel a complete resort. At night the scene is very different, it is all bright lights along the road with the tavernas, shops and restaurants vying to attract custom from the strolling crowds.

Rhodes town lies straight ahead but motorists crossing over to the east coast and wishing to avoid Rhodes town can turn right at the traffic lights outside the Rodos Palace Hotel. At the top of the hill turn right and keep ahead, ignoring the complicated traffic system on the left, apart from watching for joining traffic. Keep ahead until past the large Eurospar super-market on the right then fork off left along the road signposted Asgourou. At the T junction turn left and immediately right to continue ahead. The next junction is Lindos Avenue main road where a left turn leads back to Rhodes town and a right heads south towards Faliraki and Lindos. Using this route in reverse is equally convenient but the complicated traffic system can cause confusion on first acquaintance with its cluster of no entry signs. It is nothing more than a disguised roundabout where a left with the traffic flow followed by a right and an immediate left leads down to the Rodos Palace Hotel and the coast road.

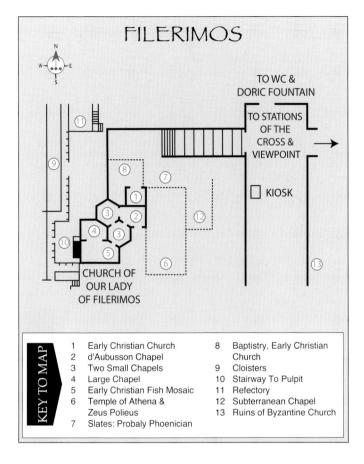

FILERIMOS

KEY TO MAP

1 Early Christian Church
2 d'Aubusson Chapel
3 Two Small Chapels
4 Large Chapel
5 Early Christian Fish Mosaic
6 Temple of Athena & Zeus Polieus
7 Slates: Probaly Phoenician
8 Baptistry, Early Christian Church
9 Cloisters
10 Stairway To Pulpit
11 Refectory
12 Subterranean Chapel
13 Ruins of Byzantine Church

Additional Information

Places to Visit

Monolithos Castle
Monolithos
Open site, no admission charge.

Kritinia Castle
Kritinia
Open site, no admission charge.

Ancient Kamiros
Open: daily 08.30am - 3.00pm, closed Monday.
There is an admission charge every day except on Sunday in winter when it is free.

Filerimos
Ialysos
Open: daily 08.30am - 3.00pm, closed Monday.
There is an admission charge every day except on Sunday in winter when it is free.

This tour of 125km (78 miles) explores the local colour and beauty spots in the northern sector of the island. Many of the country villages which lie inland of the coastal road are included as well as the much vaunted Valley of the Butterflies after which it is a gain of altitude for the heights of Profitis Ilias, the second highest mountain on the island.

One or two of the villages close to Rhodes town, like Maritsa and Pastida, have somehow escaped inclusion on the regular tourist trail and certainly do not feature on the ubiquitous 'round the island' tour so popular with tour operators and visitors alike. Inevitably some villagers are employed in tourism bringing wealth into the village, but a visit still provides an insight into life and customs of village folk. It is here where the openness, the inquisitiveness and the friendliness of the ordinary Greek people emerges if time is taken to sit and relax amongst them.

Rhodian countryside is at its brightest and most colourful in spring but the softly pine clad hills around Profitis Ilias remain refreshingly green throughout, defying the scorching heat of summer which turns lowlands into an arid desert of dried vegetation. The mountain roads are mostly well surfaced, as are the roads throughout this tour except in a few parts.

Leave Rhodes Town by the Lindos road and, once past the Koskinou junction, look for the turn off on the right to **Kalithies** for the first port of call. Situated in a hollow just out of sight of the sea, Kalithies wraps itself around a cross roads where much of the village life takes place. The bars, kafeneons and old shops add atmosphere but do not expect to find good Greek food, at least not in summer. Kalithies is the dormitory for Faliraki workers and its population includes a fair number of expatriates who started as summer workers but have now settled in the village.

For the onward route to Psinthos, turn sharp left at the cross roads in the centre of the village and shortly right following the signs. From here it is a run through quiet countryside where the road winds and twists through small interior valleys turning again when confronted by another hillock. Ignore the road off left to Afandou after 5km (3.1 miles) and keep meandering towards **Psinthos**, reached after a further 6km (3.75 miles). A huge central square overlooked by the church and several tavernas dominates the village. It and Pastides have become favoured villages for organised Greek evenings, especially in early season before Embonas warms up enough in the evening to provide competition. The road to the **Valley of the Butterflies**, the next port of call, is signposted off to the right just before the village square is reached. Climbing gradually, the road wends through pine woods to reach **Moni Kalopetra**, startlingly white in the glare of the sun, before descending to the Valley of the Butterflies. It is possible to park at the monastery and enter the valley from the upper entrance, the downside being the hike back up from the bottom. The monastery itself has a peaceful courtyard with picnic tables where the countryside can be overlooked in quiet contemplation, perhaps with a drink since light refreshments are available.

Descent through the woodlands leads very shortly to the car park for **Petaloudes**, the Valley of the Butterflies. Densely wooded and penetrated by a trickling stream, this valley is the summer resting place of an attractive butterfly (or rather moth, see feature on p.126) and they normally arrive by their thousands. It is a beauty spot in its own right and has been managed as such with walkways, waterfalls, rock pools, rustic bridges and resting places. Petaloudes is open for virtually the whole of the tourist season even though the butterflies are only actually present from late June until the end of August.

From the car park the valley runs both uphill and down with the major section uphill from the pay box. There is a restaurant /café

Petaloudes to Moni Kalopetra on Foot

This short walk explores the Valley of the Butterflies and continues beyond to wind up to the Monastery where refreshments can be taken before heading back the same way. The walk is on fairly good footpaths but sensible shoes or trainers are strongly recommended. Allow around 1 hour for the complete walk.

From the pay box at the Valley of the Butterflies set off uphill following the footpaths through this densely shaded valley. Keep on the main footpath by the stream, constantly ascending through the valley. Rise onto a track and stay on the paved path to the right, which continues left up steps to reach the upper entrance and snack bar. Stay right on the paved path across the track and up steps to meet the road at a wooden gate. From here, a left and right leads to the monastery. Return the same way. As a change from butterflies, the largest Ostrich farm and park in Greece lies on the right just 1.5km/0.9miles after leaving Petaloudes. (See opposite page).

complex at the lowest level.

From here fast roads are used to proceed towards the mountain area of Profitis Ilias. Head downhill, past the **Ostrich Farm** on the right (See box below), through Kalamon, to reach the west coast and turn left. Follow the coast road through Soroni and be prepared to turn left towards Apollona once through the town. Drive this road through light cultivation keeping an eye open for the left turn just 3.7km (2.3 miles) along for **Ag. Soulas** (St Silas). Although the chapel might be tiny, the grounds are extensive with a taverna, a large playground, football/basketball pitch and a race track! The taverna opens infrequently, usually high days, holidays and any time a crowd gathers. Crowds do gather, especially on 29-30th July, the chapel's saints day, for a large festival which includes a major attraction unique on the island, **horse racing!**

Continuing towards Dimilia, watch out for the stabilised track/road on the right leading to **Salakos**, it is reached just 5.4km (3.4 miles) after rejoining the road from the monastery. This route soon reveals views of the cypress and pine wooded Profitis Ilias and of the Italianate buildings near the summit soon to be visited. It takes a careful scrutiny to pick out the zig-zag path ascending the side of the mountain from Salakos towards the summit buildings. This is an old *kalderimi*, cobbled path, which was once the main route for taking provisions to the top by donkey and is now a popular route for walkers. See the feature on p.128 for details.

When the track/road meets the road turn left for Salakos which is soon reached.

Salakos has a small platea alongside the main road. Shaded by trees, it is a great place to twiddle the worry beads and sit in contemplation of the world and its people. The onward route out west is graced by the wooded slopes of the mountain rising away to the left where cypress slowly gives way to pine. Turn left after 5km (3.1 miles) and continue climbing to drive on the highest road on the island

Rhodes Ostrich Farm & Park

Billed as the largest Ostrich Farm in Greece, a visit here could provide a good lunchtime stop after a visit to the Valley of the Butterflies. A restaurant and a snack bar offer the opportunity to sample tasty ostrich steaks and burgers as well as an ostrich egg omelette. Other birds and animals, mainly from Asia and Australia, share the farm with the ostriches and there is also a children's playground. Open 9am - 7.30pm daily.

Butterflies of the Valley

There is no argument that the butterflies are really moths but this tiny deception pays handsomely since a Valley of the Moths title lacks that air of romanticism to draw the crowds. Fortunately, the red and black Jersey tiger moth, *Euplagia quadripunctaria*, is attractive and has the distinction of being the only moth in the world to become a major tourist attraction. Thousands arrive in the height of summer, July and August, settling on the tree trunks and on the mossy rocks for a period of aestivation but this resting is frequently disturbed by the coach loads of visitors clapping their hands to watch the cloud of moths rise from the trees. This continual disturbance has led to a reduction in the numbers returning to the valley in recent years and noisy activities, like clapping and the blowing of whistles are banned.

Why the moths come to this particular valley has never been clearly understood. Certainly the valley offers the moths a cool moist haven but the particular trees present, *Liquidambar orientalis*, which also thrives in the damp conditions, are believed to be important. These trees, exude drops of 'liquid amber' sweet gum from the bark which may attract them.

The trees are often wrongly referred to as styrax or storax but this may arise from a confusion with the closely related *Liquidambar styraciflua*, a North American native, which is called styrax or storax. To add to the confusion *Styrax officinalis*, a white flowered shrub also called styrax or storax, does grow on Rhodes but not necessarily in this valley.

Above left: Church, Elousa. *Above right:* Dimilia Church
Below left: Children waiting to go into school, Maritsa
Below right: Maritsa

Salakos to Profitis Ilias by Kalderimi

This most direct route from Salakos to the top of Profitis Ilias follows an old *kalderimi,* cobbled trail, which wends its way up the mountain side. Even though there is a fair ascent involved, the generous sweeps of the zig-zag ensure that no section is particularly steep and the walking is fairly easy.

Starting from the platea in the centre of Salakos, follow the main road out west towards Embonas until past the restaurant/hotel on the left reached after just a few minutes. From here look for a narrow concrete road on the left just where the main road bends sharply right and just before the bus shelter. Follow the narrow road for just over a minute to locate a rough track leading off to the left, just after a long white wall. This track heads straight up in the direction of the mountain and soon becomes fenced on the left. Follow the path/trail left along the top edge of the fence, just before reaching a small white shrine also on the left. Pass through a fenced gate, making sure to leave it closed, and continue on the firmly established trail. All that is necessary now is to follow through the cypress and pine trees that cloak the landscape catching views down to Salakos from time to time.

Amongst the scent of pine, spring walkers can enjoy a feast of wild flowers like the dainty white cyclamen, *C. repandum* which can be found in bloom from March at the lower levels through until late May at the top or a feast of wild orchids like the elegant, slender *Orchis anatolica* or the strikingly marked bee orchid, *Ophrys reinholdii*. Also found along here, and rather surprisingly since it tends to favour coastal locations, is the mandrake, *Mandragora officinalis*, often called the mystic mandrake. Its large wrinkled leaves form a rosette which lies close to the ground and its small pale blue flowers are followed by orange berries. It is a plant full of folk lore to which many properties have been assigned through the ages, including its use as an aphrodisiac which is mentioned in the bible. There is a little more of the folk lore which perhaps should not be ignored; the shriek emitted when the forked roots are pulled from the ground is a harbinger of death to those within earshot!

The chapel of St Anthony lies above but there is no clear view of it until the trail levels out at the top of the hill and starts to head away from the face. Keep the chapel on the right and once beyond keep right to join a woodland track. To visit the chapel and enjoy the solitude and views from its terrace turn right, otherwise turn left and follow the woodland track until the monastery of Profitis Ilias comes into view. Head for this and from here the main buildings on the top are all accessible. Return down to Salakos by the same route.

through green and flower decked fields towards the summit of Profitis Ilias. Park when the chalet buildings are reached.

Profitis Ilias, after the Prophet Elijah, is not just the name of the monastery but of the mountain and the settlement on top. The two adjacent Swiss Chalet style hotels, Elafos (stag) and Elafina (doe), were built by the Italians. Now looking distinctly jaded, they have actually been closed since 1991 but, in spite of this, they still manage to find their way into hotel lists for the island. In front of the hotels was, appropriately, a deer enclosure. The walled-in monastery itself is small and shows little signs of life until 20th June, its Saint's day.

Uphill of the road, the large chalet building which was built for the Italian Governor now stands deserted with its doors and windows flapping in the breeze. To the right is a small chapel; from the chapel it is possible to follow the footpaths laid out by the Italians in a circular walk up and along the summit ridge, for sparkling views over Apollona, and down again at the eastern end. The summit itself, occupied by the army, is not accessible. Steps from the road side lead into the small café which serves the finest yoghurt and honey on the island and there is no more relaxing place to enjoy it than on the wooden terrace outside.

Plans are afoot to restore the complex starting with the 72 room Hotel Elefos. A consortium of eight local villages has formed a company and produced a five year plan to renovate the two hotels and the Italian Governor's chalet. A huge deer park, in the woods below the hotels, is also part of the project plus other expansive schemes. It all seems a mammoth undertaking for a group of enthusiastic villagers but stranger things have happened!

At this altitude, the wild flowers can be enjoyed a little later into the season than at lower levels and it is possible to see *Cyclamen repandum*, which is widespread up here, until late May and possibly later in a cool spring. One speciality to look out for which is fairly common here but not in other parts of the island, is the charming, white *Paeonia clusii ssp rhodia*. It flowers in April and May and can sometimes be seen on the banks overhanging the road.

The onward drive to Eleousa through the cool, green forests passes the 14th century Byzantine church of **Agios Nikolaos Foundoukli** (St Nicholas of the hazelnuts) with its interesting wall paintings. It is believed that the hillsides here were once covered with hazelnuts. A pleasant place to linger with picnic tables and a small children's playground.

Entering **Eleousa**, a road system guides traffic through the old Italianate Plaza, now a crumbling edifice. Built originally as a palace for the governor, it later became a barracks for Greek troops and part of it still is used by the military. Situated on the slopes of the summit region, Eleousa offers a shady platea with a number of tavernas and snack bars which sometimes attract tour coaches.

Archipoli is the next port of call and the road there is still flanked

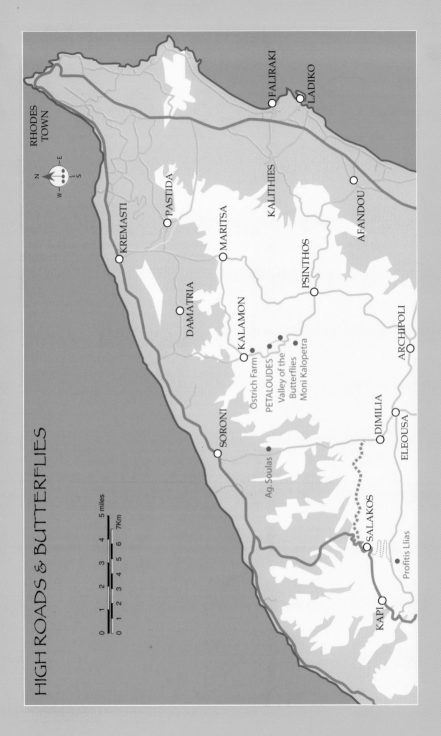

HIGH ROADS & BUTTERFLIES

RHODES TOWN

FALIRAKI
LADIKO

KALITHIES

PASTIDA

AFANDOU

KREMASTI

MARITSA

PSINTHOS

DAMATRIA

ARCHIPOLI

KALAMON

Ostrich Farm
PETALOUDES
Valley of the Butterflies
Moni Kalopetra

DIMILIA

SORONI

ELEOUSA

Ag. Soulas

SALAKOS

Profitis Llias

KAPI

5 miles

7Km

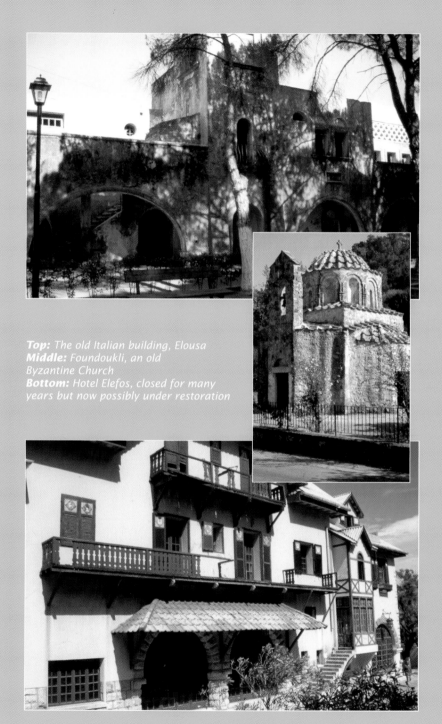

Top: *The old Italian building, Elousa*
Middle: *Foundoukli, an old Byzantine Church*
Bottom: *Hotel Elefos, closed for many years but now possibly under restoration*

by pines. A petrol station is the first building encountered providing a chance to fill up; it is one of the few around in these mountain villages. Archipoli was designed to serve the traveller. It sits astride the road offering cafés and tavernas to the wayfarer. The ochre church with its wedding cake style campanile fights for its own space amongst the houses.

On leaving Archipoli, watch out for the left turn to Psinthos in 4km (2.5 miles). A scenic run through descending foothills occasionally crosses narrow bridges and there is little sign of habitation until nearing Psinthos. Continue through Psinthos on the road to Maritsa. The route winds back up into the mountains which shelters Petaloudes and the scenery is reminiscent of it in parts. Although short, this is one of the most scenic runs on the island as the road flirts in high drama around mountain tops revealing glimpses down to lower regions from time to time.

The Pine Processionary Caterpillar

The nests seen dripping from pine trees both here and along many of the Mediterranean coasts and islands in Greece are full of the Pine Processionary Caterpillar, *Thaumetopoea pityocampa*. They live in these communal nests through the winter and come out to feed only when the weather is warm enough. Their communal behaviour persists even on leaving the nest and they move in procession, each one in contact nose to tail with the next to form chains extending to several metres in length. When fully grown, which is usually by late spring or early summer, they pupate in cocoons below ground and emerge as moths later in the summer. Eggs are laid in large numbers around the pine needles and are covered by scales from the body of the female. The reproductive cycle is completed in the course of one year.

A word of warning; these dark brown caterpillars are covered in hairs which are highly irritant and will cause a painful rash if they come into contact with the skin.

Caterpillar nest

Maritsa is one of those places tempting only to drive straight through since it seems to have no identifiable centre. It must be explored on foot. The back streets provide some of those images which are characteristically Greek, flower pots on whitewashed steps, blue doors, flower decked balconies and outside ovens. A one-way system operates through this very neat village which even boasts a block paved main street.

The tour concludes with a visit to **Pastida** before returning to Rhodes town. Pastida is now another of those dormitory villages supported by tourism without being directly engaged in it.

On entering Pastida, pass underneath the road which crosses the island to the airport. For Rhodes town head towards Kremasti and the coast road. For east coast destinations, turn right alongside a large taverna on a corner in the centre. Follow this road and stay ahead on joining the airport road towards the east coast. Pass the **Bee Keeping Museum** on the right before meeting the main Lindos road mid way between the Koskinou junction to the north and the Kalithies junction to the south.

Additional Information

Places to Visit

Valley of the Butterflies (Petaloudes) Open: 8.00am - 7.00pm. There is an entrance charge during the holiday season but free at other times.

A circuit around the skirts of Mt. Ataviros, the highest mountain range on the island, a visit to Embonas, the highest village, a chance to taste wines and a couple of monasteries are amongst the highlights on this 180km (112.5 mile) tour. Although well surfaced roads are used in the main, there is one stretch, Ag Isidoros to Laerma which is only stabilised track and slower to drive. The track is not recommended after heavy rain.

The central part of the island exists on an uneasy alliance between forestry, small scale farming and animal husbandry. Much of the region is covered by forest or scrubland with only a few areas suitable for farming. From the commercial point of view, the forests are not luxurious enough for exploitation and they provide relatively small amounts of low grade timber suitable only for fuel. Often sheep and goats are the mainstay of life in these country areas and provide milk for yoghurt and cheese as well as meat. Goats will survive in areas of meagre vegetation where other livestock would fail but overgrazing by these animals is in itself destructive in not allowing regeneration so creating a vicious circle which is difficult to break and condemns the farmer to a poor living. If there is prosperity in the region then it is at Embonas. Here altitude, climatic and soil factors combine to make it the best region on the island for growing vines and here too is the location of Emery, one of two major wine manufacturers on the island and three other small wineries. Success builds upon success, Embonas' colourful village life and high location makes a focal point for tourism, particularly for round the island tours and organised Greek evenings. The sense of isolation of this central section is most keenly observed on part of the return leg from Ag. Isidoros to Lardos via Laerma.

Leave Rhodes town on the Lindos road and continue heading south past Faliraki and the Ladiko junction. The absorbing view down the coast immediately past here, of the long sweep of the bay terminating in four distinct mountains layered one on another, vies with the view of the offshore islands on the west coast as the finest on the island. The innermost mountain here marks the Kolimbia junction on the route of this tour where a right turn towards Archipoli is required. Looking across the wide river bed immediately on turning gives a momentary view of the disused old bridge which was formerly the route of the main road. The river bed is followed up the valley for a time until past the Epta Pigis turn off. If this was not visited in Chapter 2, there is another opportunity now. Woodlands start to enclose the road as it winds in gentle ascent and leads almost unexpectedly to a large car park in front of the **Monastery of Ag. Nektarios.**

A large hollow *Platanos orientalis* tree stands before an archway which leads to steps up to the grandiose Byzantine style church guarded by columnar cypress trees. The separate campanile, with a tiered construction, is borrowed from a later period. Picnic tables are provided just outside the church and there is also a taverna/café/bar. A notice board in the car park illustrates two walks which the energetic might like to try. One heads uphill behind the monastery to two view points and the other leads from the car park down through the woods to the river bed. See also the feature below.

Pine forest still dominates the onward journey which leads through Archipoli (visited in Chapter 6) and on to Eleousa. Turn left here, through the large Italianate square and past Ag Elousa church, towards Apollona keeping south of the main Profitis Ilias summit region while heading towards the distant, barren massive of Ataviros. A dip in the road, a bend and tiny **Platania** with its striking church is passed before there is time for a glance. The eye-

Ag. Nektarios

Ag. Nektarios is a modern day saint. He was born as Anastasi Kephalas in Thrace in 1846 and died November 9th 1920.

At the age of 20 he was teaching on Chios and in 1877 he was ordained as a deacon in Alexandria and given the name of Nektarios. Following his ordination, he returned to Athens to complete his education and eventually returned to Alexandria where he was elevated to bishop in 1889.

By 1900, his health started to fail but he still managed to establish a convent for young women on the island Aegina.

Three year after his death, his body was exhumed and found preserved and sweet smelling. It remained this way for a further 20 years and when his body finally decayed, his bones remained fragrant. He was declared a saint in 1961.

There are a number of churches on Rhodes dedicated to him.

catching Byzantinesque white church of St Peter and Paul on the right distracts from the Laerma junction on the left. Laerma is visited on this tour but by a different route so it is straight on to Apollona for now. **Apollona** is altogether a more substantial village and one worth a stop to look around. Outside ovens are still used for cooking and baking bread and are particularly active around Easter time. Amongst a cluster of tavernas at the far end of the village, the more rustic Panorama Restaurant is the place to sample some oven cooked food. From the centre of the village, a paved road leads downhill signposted to the **church of Timeos Stavros** and **Folk Museum**. (Open 9am-3pm daily; closed Sunday. April - October.) The displays in this excellent museum are housed in a traditional village house complex in the garden of which are also finds from Roman sites in the locality.

Grey, imposing **Ataviros**, a mountain with a fierce presence but without character, dominates the skyline with onward progress towards Embonas. It is a mountain which does not invite walkers, it challenges them and many take up the challenge tackling it from the north west side, just beyond Embonas of which more shortly. Turn left at the junction reached 8km (5 mile) on from Apollona for the final run into **Embonas**. The first major building on the right, on entering the village is the **Emery wine factory** who are happy to receive visitors between 9.00am and 3.20pm on weekdays. Drive in through the main gate and park in the big yard, enter the factory through the main door and walk the length of the shed past all the stainless steel vats and turn right at the end into the bar reception area. Here casual visitors can enjoy a complimentary wine tasting session at the bar whereas groups have special tables set aside for them. The quieter times for casual visitors are before 10am and after 2.00pm; between these hours is a succession of coach parties. For wine buffs, there are three small traditional family wineries also in the village one of which brews the local fire-water 'souma'. They are all easy to locate once past the large Emery winery. Look carefully for Alexandris and Kounaki, both on the left before reaching the centre and Merkouris, the last building on the left leaving Embonas travelling south. All produce a range of wines and are open for wine tasting. Souma distillation takes place at the Merkouris winery and is made from the wine residues. A good time to see some action is at the end of summer when the grapes are harvested.

Embonas, the village, has a disproportionate number of tavernas for its size. It is famed on the island for the quality of its meat which makes it a natural target for a lunch stop, either before or after wine tasting, on every single round-the-island tour offered. Many coaches are back again in the evening for the organised Greek evening so popular with holidaymakers. The village has blossomed both tavernas and tourist shops to satisfy the passing trade. For the casual visitor, it is

Churches & Monasteries

Throughout a long and turbulent history, the church on Rhodes has been at the heart of society and provided an enduring constancy which bonds people even today. Its buildings themselves, many from the 13th and 14th century or earlier, offer a strand of historical and social comment but equally fascinating is the difference in architectural styles which have developed in its isolation from Greece, styles which are not seen elsewhere outside the Dodecanese.

The most obvious of these is the tiered campanile standing separately from the main church building and sometimes used as the entrance gate. Simpler examples, like Moni Skiadi, have just two tiers under a small roof dome, but those on a grander scale, and one of the best examples is at Archangelos, may have six or seven ever decreasing tiers. Almost invariably white, they offer one of the lasting impressions of the island. Another fairly distinctive feature is the cross-vaulting in the roof and few of the modern churches are without it.

Religious pilgrimage is a major form of tourism amongst the Greek people who are prepared to travel island to island to see famous ikons or monasteries. Many of the monasteries now recognise this and are responding by building overnight accommodation within the grounds, as at Moni Thari. Even the most humble of the churches and monasteries recognise their social role and encourage their grounds to be used to celebrate festivals and name days and facilities for this are never neglected when expansion plans are in the air.

Myth, folklore and religion are intertwined on Rhodes more than anywhere in Greece and many of the saints are quite local and completely without pedigree. In much the same way, many local customs and superstitions are built in to religious ritual and some of these, like the belief in the evil eye, are a legacy left behind by the Turks.

Moni Thari

Emery Wines

Located at the heart of the vine region on the island, Emery is on hand to work closely with the farmers in advising and selecting vineyards which produce the most suitable grapes. The region around Embonas is cooled by altitude and by winds funnelled from the west which produce very local microclimates. Throw the soil factor into the equation and the result is that particular vineyards in the region are superior to others in the quality of grape produced. Two grape varieties are prominent here, the Athiri grape for the white wine and the Amorgianos for the red. Like other wine growers on the island, they are trying their hand with Cabernet Sauvignon.

Harvest time lasts around three weeks, from late August into September and the subsequent fermentation stage also lasts about 2/3 weeks. The white wine is ready in one year but the better quality red wine (Cava) is stored in oak casks for six months bottled and stored for up to three years. Italian wine tasters are used to help maintain quality.

Their wine list includes;

Emery Villare: served chilled, this is an excellent dry, slightly fruity wine which, at its price, is the best of the island's white wines.
Athiri: another excellent dry white wine with plenty of character.
Granrose Emery: a rosé wine, again very good.
Rodon: a Cabernet Sauvignon which will make its mark amongst the island's red wines.

They also produce sparkling white wines and, of course, ouzo.

Yamas! (cheers!)

Above: *Grapes on the vine.*
Inset: *Alexandris, wine producer, Embonas*

Wild Orchids of Rhodes

The island is blessed with a rich orchid flora which graces the spring months from March, and perhaps earlier for one or two species, through until late May. These are the terrestrial orchids which have their bulbous roots in the ground and not the exotic epiphytics of hotter, steamier climes which are popular for greenhouse cultivation.

In distribution the orchids are just about everywhere where cultivation and grazing pressure allows. Mostly, they have a preference for limestone geology so these regions have a greater number of species. Even so, some areas on the island are richer in orchids than others. One of these is alongside the road to Epta Pigis, close to the Kolimbia junction and another is the summit area around Profitis Ilias. Altitude has a significant influence on flowering times so the sea level site near Kolimbia junction, for example, needs to be explored in March and early April whilst the cooler high altitude site at Profitis Ilias might yield orchid discoveries into late May. For those who thrill at finding wild orchids, the best two weeks when the greatest number of species are in flower at the same time is the first two in April although there is some small seasonal variation.

Orchids have a remarkably consistent botanical structure which irritates the botanist because the usual technique of flower identification, a detailed examination of the reproductive parts followed by the application of a diagnostic key, does not apply so readily. To the absolute delight of the lay man, the best course lies in matching with a picture so with a good book in hand, like Pierre Delforge's **Photo Guide to Orchids of Britain and Europe (Collins)**, and with a little experience it is easy to become an expert.

The island's 50 or so species are dominated by the bee orchids (genus *Ophrys*) and the genus *Orchis*. Bee orchids, with each flower resembling some species of bee or wasp, are usually the most difficult to spot. Often not taller than 23cm (9in), their slender stems carrying perhaps three or four flowers blend in amongst the vegetation with ease. Almost as difficult to spot are the slender spikes of the *Orchis* genus but with a good array of flowers they can be more eye-catching.

Some of the island's orchids which are not difficult to find are listed below:

Genus *Ophrys*:

O. fusca
O. sicula
O. tenthredinifera
O. iricolour
O. omegaifera
O. vernixia

O. mammosa
O. scolopax
O. bornmulleri
O. regis-ferdinandii
O. holoserica
O. heldreichii
O. reinholdii
O. ferrum-equinum

Continued from p140

Genus Orchis:

O. papilionacea
O. anatolica
O. italica
O. provincialis
O. lactea
O. laxiflora
O. coriophora
O. sancta

Others:

Aceras anthropophorum
Anacamptis pyramidalis
Barlia robertiana
Limodorum arbortivum
Neotinea maculata
Serapias bergonii
Serapias orientalis
Serapias parviflora

extremely difficult to find a quiet spot for lunch for a couple of hours following midday. One place to try is the Hasapotaverna, the butcher's taverna. To find it on foot head up the taverna lined street towards the church and the Bakis Brothers' Hasapotaverna lies just past and to the left with part outside the butchers shop and more over the road. By car, look for the sign to the taverna and car park off left on leaving the village heading south. The only way to capture some of the character of the village is to wander the narrow streets around the church where an interesting small **folk museum** is also situated. Winter is the time for villagers to concentrate on their handicrafts, particularly lace and hand made carpets, which are prominent in the tourist shops throughout summer.

Continue the tour by driving through Embonas heading out towards the west coast. Just outside, particularly where a track runs off left, is one of the more spectacular views of the steep face of Mt. Ataviros. Looking at the face of the mountain, there are three gulley-like depressions descending from near the summit and the route for walkers climbs up the central one. It takes almost three hours to reach the top and a similar time to come down but it is not a walk for the inexperienced. At the top, and which few people get to see, are the remains of a temple dedicated to Zeus. Built of local stone, it blends so well it is almost imperceptible but the most significant part is a side wall built in large rectangular blocks.

Where the road forks, on the way to join the coast road, keep left which is effectively ahead. Both roads actually lead to the coast road and the one to the right is useful for those heading north. Turn left on reaching the coast road and spare a moment to enjoy the view of the offshore islands north to south, and nearest, are the small islands of Makri, Strongili and Tragoussia; still north to south, more distant and larger are Alimnia

Left: *Iconostasis, Ag. Sofia
& Irene, near Laerma*
Below: *Ag. Sofia & Irene,
near Laerma*

Mount Ataviros

and Halki. It is one of the finest viewpoints on the island and the vision of those islands floating in a colour wash of blue is almost surreal. There is more than one occasion to enjoy the offshore views on the run south before the turn off left to **Ag. Isidoros**, after 6.2km (3.9 miles). It is a good road which winds around the contours all the way to Ag. Isidoros. This is a small village built on the steep lower slopes of Mt. Ataviros and full of snack bars. It is so steeply tiered in places that a walk down through the village gives mostly views of roof tops and chimneys and, in places, it is easily possible to walk from the street straight onto a flat roof. If the Papas is around, there is little chance of avoiding a visit to the church to see the finely carved pulpit bearing the name of the craftsman. So enthusiastic is the Papas, he seems totally oblivious to dress which other churches would regard as improper!

Once through Ag. Isidoros, look for the track right leading to Laerma. Progress slows for the next 11km (6.9 miles) until Laerma is reached. Although in the main the track is good, there are parts which are rough and need to be taken slowly. It is a slow, steady descent through one of the more remote regions of the island. Nearing Laerma, the church of **Ag. Sophia and Irene** enjoys a commanding view over the countryside. Cradled in the hills in splendid isolation, Laerma, with a population of around 650, is only slightly smaller than Ag. Isidoros. Turn right in the centre of the village for a short side trip to one of the ecclesiastical treasures of the island, **Moni Thari**. There is a signposted left fork to reach the monastery, dedicated to the Archangel Michael, which was built around the 13th century on much earlier foundations and offers some fine, old frescos. The north and south walls are the oldest, 12th century, part of the building but some ninth century remains can be seen in the surrounding grounds. The dome, the apse and the nave all carry frescos of exceptional crafts-manship. Some parts of the wall have as many as four layers of painting, the earliest from AD-1100. The apse has three layers. Centuries after construction, it has expanded to include accommod-ation for the many, usually Greek, pilgrims who visit the site. It is a quiet and tempting place to picnic with facilities on hand, unless there is a festival in full swing and May 21/22nd is one of those occasions.

And it is back to Laerma which has the distinction of being the village closest to the geographical centre of the island. Well outside Laerma, the fields on the right are damp and boggy in winter and spring providing the ideal habitat for certain flowers which are found nowhere else on the island. The most prominent and eye-catching of these is a tall-growing purple orchid, *Orchis laxiflora* which grows here in abundance. Rhodes is particularly well blessed with wild orchids and more details are given in the feature on p.140.

The road follows a ridge for a time affording excellent views over a landscape once devastated by forest fires but now regenerating. On entering Lardos head right for a side trip to Moni Ipseni. Signposts lead the way through the woodland. Stations of the cross are first glimpsed through the trees and shortly afterwards the monastery is reached. It is of recent construction and unusual in that it is a living, working monastery in the control of an order of nuns. Cool elegance awaits with citrus trees surrounding a fountain in the quiet courtyard. Outside is a large area used for festivities and a white chapel overlooks from a nearby hill.

Return to Lardos and rejoin the coastal road for the journey back to Rhodes Town. If time is not pressing, try the existing sections of the National Road which are a little slower to drive but scenically more interesting. The first section starts off left north of Kalathos and leads through Massari and Malona to Archangelos. Almost immediately on rejoining the main coast road, look again for a left turn which has a sign for Savas Pottery and Rhodes.

Additional Information

Places to Visit

Emery wine factory
Open: weekdays 9.00am - 3.20pm

Moni Thari
Open: not always open but available for viewing if someone is around.

Moni Ipseni
Open: no regular opening hours but the most reliable time is in the morning.

T his tour of 242km (151 miles) explores the lesser visited southernmost section of the island. The eastern coast road, generally much quicker than the western route, is used for both access and the return. Allow about 1.5 hours for the drive down from Rhodes Town to Gennadi which is effectively the start of the tour. Although villages feature strongly in this tour, two of the most remarkable beaches on the island are also visited, one at Plimmiri and the other at island's end, Prasonissi, now a magnet for wind and kite surfers where the sea laps in from both sides.

High mountains are left behind for hills and plains largely given over to cultivation. Farming is the chief industry of all the villages in the region but agriculture on the island has been a struggle throughout the ages. Many factors have contributed to this: the inability to harness the high winter rainfall for summer irrigation, soil erosion, small plots arising from the necessity for equal land division according to inheritance law and the lack of mechanisation. Under the Italian regime, the Italians tried hard to tackle these problems and a large scale model farm was set up outside Katavia, where the buildings are still to be seen, and staff brought from Italy to teach modern farming methods. Metal windmills were introduced to help recover deep water for irrigation, still seen in some parts of the island, and encouragement was given to increase the usage of fertilisers and agricultural equipment. The Italians actually went much further and expropriated some of the better quality land around Malona and brought in Italian farmers to lead by example. Farming techniques are much improved now but many of the old problems still restrict production. Fields of wheat, oats and barley are common sights around Katavia but melons too are becoming an important crop in some areas, chiefly around Apolakia, and, of course the ubiquitous olive (see the feature on p.149)

Tourism has burgeoned in the southern region with the surfacing of the route down to Prasonissi which has become a mecca for water sports enthusiasts. Petrol stations are still thin on the ground so it pays to set off with a full tank but otherwise tourist facilities in the way of cafés and tavernas are not in short supply. Suggestions for a lunch stop include the hill village of Istrios, Arnitha or Katavia for a peaceful countryside location or Plimmiri and Prasonissi if a view of the sea takes precedence.

Follow the Lindos road out of Rhodes town but once through Kalathos, turn right towards Lardos and avoid driving around the Lindos headland. On reaching Gennadi turn right following signs to Apolakia. Just 7km (4.4miles) along, watch for the left turn to visit the small village of **Vati**. The pace of life is slow here and the sleeping policemen on the entry road ensure that visitors slow down too. There is room to park by the church which has a bell-tower gate. Cubic white houses scattered to some predetermined configuration contrive to leave room for a shady village square. Here is a beautiful spot to enjoy a drink or have lunch at 'O Petrino' or 'Platonas' tavernas under the gaze of a few elderly residents idly toying with their worry beads. This quiet backwater is another world and bearing testament to this scene of inactivity are the ruins of a windmill on a nearby hill.

Back on the main road, entertained perhaps by the electric blue flashes of swooping bee-eaters which are particularly common in this area, the next turn to look out for is a right turn up to the villages of Profilia and Istrios. These lie on a loop road which climbs high into the hills passing through both these villages before rejoining this same main road. It is a steady climb on a good road through a regenerating forest area. **Profilia**, snuggling in the saddle of a hill and tucked well away from invaders' eyes, is revealed with gaining altitude. White village houses tumble around the hillsides and outside

ovens suggest that the way of life is still fairly traditional. From the cool surroundings of the church there are views over to Mt. Ataviros. Expansive views on the descent to Istrios encompass the Akramitis range of hills and the village of Siana on its slopes. Cereal crops, golden in the summer sun, have no respect for altitude here. **Istrios**, small and compact, has a large platea which is easily by-passed but is the best place to park. Stay ahead on entering the village, where the road bends left by a café/bar on the right, to the centre. 'El Greco' looks an interesting place to eat and boasts Greek specialities as well as an international menu. Turn right by the café/bar at the village entrance and it is the next building on the right. From here it is 6km (3.75 miles) back to the Apolakia road and, almost immediately after turning right to join it, turn left for the village of **Arnitha**.

On the left, just before entering the village, is a shady courtyard with a drinking fountain and a taverna which is a quiet place to dine except on a Sunday when the Greeks themselves are out in force. Opposite to this courtyard is the small chapel of Ag. Nektarios. Heading into the village still, the **Monastery of Ag. Filemonos** with its large courtyard lies along a road to the left. Before the road bends right to head into the village proper, there is a track ahead which connects Arnitha to Mesanagros but is only suitable for four wheel drive vehicles with good clearance. Arnitha itself climbs a steep hillside and is another of those villages best explored on foot to capture all

The Olive

Known from Crete as early as 3,500BC, the olive has been central to the existence of the Mediterranean peoples for millennia. Although grown primarily for oil for cooking, the oil is also used as a lubricant, for lighting, soap making and in ointments and liniments for the skin. The fruit itself, the olive, is also eaten.

The tree is evergreen with leathery lance-shaped leaves which are dark green above and silvery beneath. With age the trunks become knarled and twisted adding considerably to the character of the tree. It takes 4-8 years for a tree to start bearing fruit but full production is not reached until after 15-20 years and it may then continue for centuries with proper care. The tree is erratic in that not every year produces a good crop, unless a suitable regime of irrigation and feeding is rigorously followed, but more often good crops are expected every other year. Whitish flowers borne in loose clusters arrive in late and which rely on the wind for pollination. The fruit which follows takes 6-8 months to reach full maturity for only then does it give the maximum yield of oil. This means that harvesting takes place throughout the winter months, from December through until March, the perfect complement to working in the tourist season. Fruits for eating are collected before maturity and need special treatment with dilute caustic lye and salt to kill the extreme bitterness. There are hundreds of named varieties of olives, both for oil and for eating, which are propagated from hard wood cuttings or from leaf cuttings under mist propagation.

Olive oil is produced in a selection of grades, the very finest oil from the first pressing is known as virgin oil and this is the grade preferred for salad dressing. It is a good buy to take home too and it can be found on supermarket shelves in 5 litre containers. The second grade of oil is the pure, a blend of virgin oil and refined oil, which is the third grade. Refined oil is made from the lampante grade, so called because it is used for lamp fuel, by treatment to remove the acid, the colour and the odour. Lampante is obtained from a second pressing of the residual pulp.

The wood too is of great value. It is very hard, strongly grained and takes a fine polish, ideal for carving, cabinet work and toys. It is good too as a slow burning fuel and for making charcoal for which the Greeks have a great demand.

Botanically, the olive, *Olea europea*, belongs to the Oleaceae family and has some interesting and familiar relatives like ash, privet, jasmine and lilac.

Rockroses

There is a view that Rhodes takes its name from the rose but these are not native to the island. Rockroses, belonging to the genus *Cistus,* are native and they thrive in the hot dry conditions found more particularly in the south. Since there are only three species growing on Rhodes, identification poses no real problems. Two are pink and the other, the sage-leaved cistus, *C. salviifolius*, is white. Separating the two pink ones is done simply on the size of the flower, *C. creticus* has the larger flower and *C. parviflorus* the smaller. Sometimes, when the two are not close for immediate comparison, and the size alone is no help then the next guide is to look at the central style. If this is equal in length to the stamens then it is *C. creticus*, if shorter it is the small flowered one.

Individually, the flowers are short lived surviving usually for only one day. The first flush of flowers in spring sees the bushes covered in bloom for a time but later in the season the flowers are much reduced in number. Often they manage to stay in flower with just one or two flowers showing until well into summer.

Herbs and plants are intertwined in the lives and culture of the Mediterranean peoples and many have their own story to tell. This is certainly true of *Cistus creticus* which has provided gum ladanum, highly valued in perfumery. The gum exudes from the plant and sticks to the legs and beards of goats as they graze on and amongst the bushes. One way that has been used to collect the gum is to patiently comb it from the goat's beard. The other relies on a little more help from man and was carried out by monks into the middle ages. A kind of leather rake was dragged over the leaves of the plant in the midday heat when the extrusion of gum takes place and the resin then gathered from the rake.

Rock roses, Citrus creticus

OFF THE BEATEN TRACK SOUTHERN VILLAGES

those cameos of flower decked doorways and balconies which are so characteristically Greek.

On the outskirts of Apolakia, visited in Chapter 4, a narrow road goes off right to Varda Dam. This 4km (2.5 miles) diversion leads along a narrow road through melon growing country to a large dam, passing a small track off left to Moni Georgios Varda. There are expansive views from the dam and four-wheel drive vehicles can continue on to Siana. Apolakia may appear to be only a cluster of café/restaurants at the junction with the east coast but, like most villages, it is best explored on foot. Turn left at the central junction towards Katavia. Melon fields are on view around Katavia, one of the major melon growing centres on the island, but civilisation is soon left behind as a wilder stretch of coastline adds a new dimension to the ever changing scenery on this island. Inland, **Moni Skiadi**, the next port of call, can be seen sitting on a ledge. Look for a left turn just 6.4km (4 miles) out from Katavia, signposted Moni Skiadi, and follow this fairly good track into the hills and up to the monastery.

Moni Skiadi is one of the more important monasteries on the island made famous by its miraculous ikon of the Blessed Virgin (Panagia). Legend tells of a heretic who stabbed the painting many centuries ago and brought blood from the cheek of Mary. Still visible brown stains provide their own persuasive evidence. The ikon is carried around at Easter time from house to house and village to village until it finally comes to rest for a period on the island of Halki. Most of the present buildings arise from the 18th and 19th centuries built around a 13th-century Church of the Holy Cross. In its present form, the tiered campanile is attached to the church building which has a typical cross vaulted roof. Rooms are available for guests wishing to stay overnight but expect it all to be full on 8th September when a panayiria is held to celebrate the birth of the Virgin Mary. People from all over the island pilgrimage to the monastery to see the miraculous ikon and to join the celebrations which go on throughout the day and night.

Retrace the route back to the coast road and continue heading south to Katavia. At the cross roads where right is signposted Prasonissi, turn left for now into **Katavia**. A short ride leads to the heart of the village, the platea, built around a road junction. Café-bars and tavernas cater for the passing tourist trade and, unless temptation is resisted, it is easy to join the Greeks, sit back in the leafy shade and watch the world go by. Those with a little energy left may prefer to wander the back streets to explore the older part of the

Church at Katavia

village. Some of the houses here have imposing doorways guarded by embedded columns.

Return back to the cross roads and stay ahead to Prasonissi. The road starts off through cultivation but this is quickly left behind as scrub takes over to dominate the landscape. White and pink rock-roses are common in the scrubland and, although perhaps more conspicuous down south, they thrive in all hot and dry locations. There are just three species on the island which are easily identified, see the feature on p.150. Although the scrubland looks most hostile to more delicate plants, a few species of wild orchid also grow here but they are only to be seen in the spring as is the small yellow *Fritillaria rhodia*.

When **Prasonissi** comes into view, it is a sight to bring progress to a temporary halt. Here east coast and west coast are separated only by a strip of sand which leads out to the headland of Prasonissi. Prasonissi, or Leek Island, possibly takes its name from the wild slliums growing there. The sand spit, which sometimes disappears under water in the storms of winter, suffers crashing walls of Aegean surf on the west side and is lapped by a gentle Mediterranean on the east. It is a great spot for windsurfers and very popular in high season. Also in the heat of summer, the sand gets compacted enough for four wheel drives to cross over to the headland but it is best not attempted in a small saloon since rescue parties are not always on hand. Prasonissi has expanded slightly since the road was surfaced and there is now a choice of tavernas, shops and accommodation but development is still very low-key. Return the same way to rejoin the main road outside Katavia. This time turn right through the gentle,

Prasonissi

Prasonissi

Below & inset left: *Plimmiri beach*

Above: Katavia. *Below:* Wheatfields near Katavia
with Agios Pavlos in the distance

cultivated landscape towards **Agios Pavlos**. It is here that the buildings of the model farm built by the Italians can still be seen but they are now disused except for storage by local farmers. Just 5km (3.1 miles) on from Agios Pavlos, there is a right turn to look out for down to Plimmiri. **Plimmiri** has a huge crescent of deserted beach backed by sand dunes borrowed from some other exotic location, probably the South Pacific. There is no village here, it is just a fishing harbour sheltered by an ugly concrete mole, a taverna and a small church. Specialising in fish, the taverna here has a good reputation and a fine position overlooking the bay. Behind the taverna, and almost part of it, is the **church of Zoodochou Pigis** which was erected on an earlier Christian basilica and incorporates some of the old pillars and marble. The church is only open 12 noon - 5pm on Sundays 1st May - 30th October. Despite the mole, it is a pleasant place for lunch and a tranquil spot to while away some time on the beach.

For the next stop, Mesanagros, return to the main road and cross directly over to join a track. It is good stabilised track which heads inland and, after 3.4km (2.1 miles), join the surfaced road by turning left to **Mesanagros**. It is a gentle climb through undulating country-side and even when Mesanagros comes into view above there is some winding up still left before the village is reached. The road flirts with rather than penetrates the village so overshoot is a distinct possibility. Park up somewhere around the sign for 'O Mike's'

taverna. If an insistent invitation of 'come, come!' rings out on setting foot outside the car, it will be Mike himself trawling for business. He is one of those larger-than-life colourful characters so beloved of travel writers and should his invitation be accepted then no doubt he will proudly display for you his collection of English newspaper cuttings in which he is mentioned. Next to Mike's taverna is the 13th-century Byzantine church of the '**Assumption of the Virgin Mary**'. If it is locked, Mike has a key and will organise someone to look after things. It is a barrel vaulted church with a pebble mosaic floor built over ruins of a fifth century Christian basilica. Over the door is the lintel from an earlier church and inside is a painted wooden screen. Evidence around suggests it is a fair mix of ages. Stroll through the village to the **church of Taxiarchis** and note how renovation of village houses is bringing a spark of life back into this sleepy backwater.

Return along the same road back to **Lahania** which is the last stop before setting off for home. Lahania was one of those villages dying on its feet until it was discovered by foreigners, mostly from Germany, and over the past decade, and even before, new residents have been buying up and restoring old property. To find the village square, unusually located at one end rather than centrally in the village, follow signs to Café Platanos. Shaded by a huge platanos tree, the café looks out onto two fountains and the village church. It is another village best explored on foot since the alleyways are particularly narrow.

Leave Lahania by continuing along the road to rejoin the coast road ready for the drive north back to Rhodes Town.

Mesanagros

Since Rhodes is well connected by air and sea, there are no end of excursions that can be planned from the island. Two of the most popular are the packaged excursions to Symi and to Marmaris in Turkey where all that is necessary is to book a ticket and turn up in time. Once at the destination the cosseting ends and many wander around waiting for the return boat totally unaware of the lost opportunities. In this chapter, some background and suggested itineraries are offered for these excursions to help fill the day profitably. Also included are two other tours, to the small island of Halki and to the larger and little visited island of Karpathos, which are easily managed from Rhodes but require a little more planning. Opportunities abound for island hopping with connections to Tilos, Nissiros and Kos. A weekly ferry connects the Aegean islands from Crete via Rhodes, Samos, Chios, Lesvos and Lemnos to the Greek mainland in the north, besides summer hydrofoil connections. It is also possible to visit Turkey taking in Marmaris, Datca, Knidos and Bodrum and returning via Kos back to Rhodes. Ferries to Pireas also offer plenty of island hopping choices.

SYMI

PRACTICAL DETAILS

Symi is a small island, one of the Dodecanese group, lying 20 miles to the north west of Rhodes close to the shores of Turkey.

Several boats leave in convoy daily from Mandraki harbour in Rhodes Town most departing at 9.00am. All the ferry boats are of a similar size and standard but the speedier catamarans and hydrofoils dominate connections to nearby islands. Catamaran and hydrofoil journeys usually cost more than normal ferry boats. If speed is essential choose the hydrofoil but remember passengers are enclosed in an airline-type cabin with limited views. For speed coupled with a sailing experience, a catamaran may be preferable. The journey time by ferry boat is a margin over two hours and less on the catamaran. Those intending to stay on Symi for a night or so can do so at no extra charge but must declare their intentions on entering the boat to get a return ticket.

Apart from stopping in the main harbour in Yialos, Symi's capital, all the boats also call in and spend around 1 hour at Panormitis to visit the monastery. Some boats call in the morning on the way and others call in the afternoon on the return. Those who prefer to spend all the time in the main harbour on Symi should ask before boarding to find out which boats will be going directly and which will make the return directly then choose accordingly.

THE ISLAND

Holidays have those unforgettable moments and sailing into Symi harbour is one. Elegant neo-classical houses in ochre, yellows and gold cascade down the grey hillsides almost spilling into the indigo pool of the harbour. A clock tower guards the quay to the right where waterside tavernas spread their awnings wide denying the sun and reflecting its rays to burnish pastel houses and to brighten grey rock. Its impact is enough to hush fellow passengers leaving the tranquillity of the moment disturbed only by a chorus of clicking camera shutters!

With only a short stay in prospect there is barely time to inspect the main harbour at **Yialos** and visit the old village **Chorio** which lies above. Yialos is the main tourist centre where, thanks to the daily influx of visitors, all the necessary facilities can be found without travelling too far. Tavernas, restaurants, snack bars, shops and sponge sellers all crowd Mourayio, the quay where the boats dock. For centuries the Symiotes have been amongst the most brave and daring sponge fishers in the Aegean. When Suleiman the Magnificent took over the Dodecanese in 1522, Symi submitted to the Sultan and offered him a choice from the island's sponges to gain privileges which allowed them to continue their mercantile trade unhindered. A quantity of the finest sponges became the annual tax on the island. Now the best of the sponges are saved for tourists, with gentle persuasion to buy the environmentally friendly natural brown sponges instead of the clear yellow bleached variety. The environmental argument is on the lines that the chemicals used to bleach sponges afterwards become pollutants and the process actually weakens the sponge and shortens its life leading to more frequent replacement. Sponges with small pores produce a creamy lather good for babies whilst the more open sponges are better for baths and showers.

Virtually all the neo-classical houses around the harbour are nineteenth century but there is some older architecture on view at Horio (Chorio). The island's strong association with ship building and the sea is honoured by a trireme carved in stone copied from Lindos on the Mourayio quayside and a **Nautical Museum**, sited at the end of the square behind the harbour, which displays models of sailing ships used in local waters, shipmakers' tools, ship and diving equipment.

Bathers often swim off the rocks just around the corner from the clock tower in front of Aliki Hotel but there is a tiny beach at **Nos**. To find the beach, continue past Hotel Aliki and follow the paved walkway which leads very shortly to Nos where a taverna guards a small shingle beach with space for about two dozen sun beds.

There are still more tavernas across the bridge at the inner end of the harbour, which are generally quieter, and narrow streets to explore especially if shopping for groceries, souvenirs, herbs or just looking for a bar.

A little further around the quay on the side opposite Mourayio, is the taxi rank. Around here too is where the minibus picks up passengers for Horio and Pedi.

Horio, the main village, lies up the hillside above Yialos and is reached by the Kali Strata, a stepped street which starts from the inner end of the harbour. Kali Strata starts modestly but soon widens to a broad street with 375 steps in short flights spaced by long slopes and with barely a shadow to protect from the heat of the midday sun. Taken at a slow pace, and provided that the roadside herb sellers do not provide a serious distraction, around 10-15 minutes is enough to reach the bars and taverna at the top which mark the start of the village proper. Both the taxi and the minibus come up to the village by a longer route.

Horio is a rambling mass of houses crowded onto a saddle and divided by a confusion of narrow twisting connecting and inter-connecting alleyways. Apart from the engaging ambience, the old apothecary, the museum and the old Kastro make the climb worthwhile.

From the shady pergola over the bar area at the top of Kali Strata, continue to climb but look on the right within a minute for the **apothecary** set back on the right. While the doctor still holds his surgery in a side room, this 19th-century pharmacy welcomes visitors to look around. Little has changed since the shop opened and the old porcelain jars store Nux Vomica or Tincture of Belladonna or extract of Digitalis on crowded shelves. There is also an old pressure pot for sterilisation, endless medicines and potions and a rather puzzling empty bottle of Scotch whisky!

Continue to climb the main street but notice now the blue signs on the wall for the **museum** which actually started right down in the harbour.

This small museum, for which entry is free, concentrates largely on the island's religious mon-uments. There are many of these with around 100 barrel vaulted chapels scattered over Symi and some in quite remote places. Photographs of the oldest chapels and their frescos are shown with concise information in Greek and English including details too of some of the island's famous religious painters.

From just a little higher than the

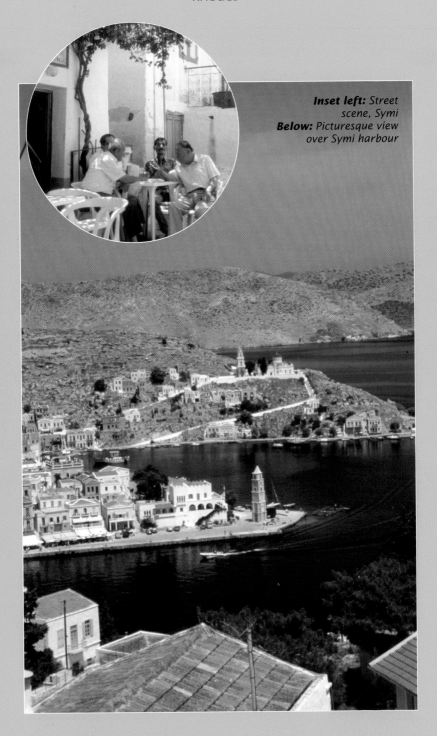

Inset left: Street
scene, Symi
Below: Picturesque view
over Symi harbour

EXCURSIONS FROM RHODES

museum, signs indicate the direction of the **Kastro** but lead only as far as the large church. From here cross below the church and keep in the same direction until the Kastro's walls come into view. Not too much remains now except the strong walls of this medieval fortress which was built over the old acropolis. Inside was a church dedicated to the Virgin Mary but this was destroyed in World War II and the nearby church of St George inherited its name.

Horio looks over the ridge westwards to the small water front village of Pedi which has the best local beach. Walking down takes around 30 minutes. Pedi has fishermen's cottages, waterside tavernas and some tourist accommodation loosely grouped at the sandy end of a deep inlet.

Panormitis, located in the extreme south-east of the island, takes around 1 hour to reach by ferry and is a highly commercialised monastery. Built in the 18th century and dedicated to Archangel Michael, the patron saint of Symi, Panormitis stands on the site of a smaller chapel with the same dedication, which was destroyed in the Middle Ages. An imposing tiered campanile guards the entrance to a black and white pebbled courtyard. The church has fine if somewhat blackened frescos and a magnificent carved wooden ikonostasis. Also there are two small museums. Alongside the church is a restaurant, accommodation and a bread shop held in high esteem by the Greeks.

THE TURKEY EXCURSION

PRACTICAL DETAILS

The destination of this trip is Marmaris which lies almost due north of Rhodes on the Turkish mainland. Ferry boats leave daily for this 2 hour journey, including the faster hydrofoil service. Tickets are available from Tourist Agencies all over the island. The cost of the excursion is extraordinarily high, inflated in part by the entry tax imposed by the Turks and reciprocated by the Greeks. Normally the Greek tax is incorporated in the price but the Turkish tax has to be paid directly on entry. It is the normal procedure to collect passports for this trip the day before departure and return them on boarding. This excursion is not simply a change of resort, it is also a change of culture. Turkey is a Moslem country and their religious day is Friday but they follow European trading practice for trade and commerce so that Friday is normal in this respect. Saturday and Sunday are treated as weekdays and the shops are all open all day so, from the point of view of planning an excursion, all days are equal. Friday, however, is market day which adds a lot of life and colour to the excursion.

MARMARIS

Marmaris is a major resort and marina on the Aegean coast of

Turkey. The boat docks close to the part that was the original fishing village, now the heart of the resort, and not far from the tourist office. There is no beach immediately on hand but the nearest is at close-by **Icmeler** which is easily reached using the frequent mini bus (dolmus) service.

The site of the Friday market is inland to the west of the landing point and best located by tracking the stream of Turks carrying great bags of fruit and vegetables back to source. Lively and colourful, just about everything is for sale from mouth-watering fruit through to plastic buckets, towels, clothing and even baby chicks. Not only is the shopping good here, it is also good in Marmaris generally and many of the Greeks themselves come over just to shop. The Turks are great salesmen but sometimes their persistence upsets first time visitors. Their technique is to engage a potential customer in polite conversation then persuade them to look at their goods. A typical opening gambit is the question 'Where are you from?' and the best way to deal with this is to make no answer if no involvement is desired.

Good buys amongst the shopping includes T-shirts and clothing in general including leather goods, onyx and honey. Honey comes in a surprising number of varieties including pine, orange, cotton, eucalyptus and general flower honey. There are a number of shops which sell tiny sampler jars or will let you try some that are already open. Orange honey is very clear and light with the faintest hint of marmalade whereas the pine honey is one of the darkest with a strong flavour. Cotton and eucalyptus might seem unlikely sources but both are delicately flavoured honeys.

And, of course, there are Turkish carpets. Working on the percentage principle, considerable powers of persuasion are used to invite visitors into the salesroom. Potential customers are treated courteously and with hospitality, usually tea, orange tea or raki, similar to the Greek ouzo. The sales pitch usually covers details of the manufacture of these hand made carpets, of the plant dyes employed and the significance of the various motifs used in the designs. A range of dazzling carpets is then displayed which tempts more than a few but the salesmen remain cheerfully philosophical and just as friendly to those who leave without buying.

If shopping and wandering around the old part of town leaves time to spare, a peaceful escape needs just a short excursion out of town to **Ataturk Parki**. This lies to the east of Marmaris and is easily reached on foot in around 15 minutes by following the coast road out past the marina. This beautiful green park lying next to the sea shore is shaded by masses of **Liquidambar orientalis** trees, the same trees found in the Valley of the Butterflies on Rhodes. Walkways lead on woodland strolls over rustic bridges to cafés and various picnic areas where it is not usually difficult to find some peace and quiet.

HALKI

PRACTICAL DETAILS

Halki is a tiny island lying roughly 10 miles off the west coast of Rhodes, just about due west of Embonas. A ferry boat provides a daily service from Halki to Skala Kamiros essentially to bring Halki residents over to Rhodes in the morning and return them in the evening. Using this service, a minimum stay of two nights needs to be spent on Halki simply to have a full day on the island. On Sunday, the ferry times make it possible to enjoy a day trip departing Kamiros Skala in the morning and returning in the evening. See the Additional Information at the end of the chapter for the actual times. One further complication is the lack of a bus service from Rhodes Town to Kamiros Skala on a Sunday which means using either a hire car or a taxi.

Ferry boats and a hydrofoil leave from Rhodes Town calling in at Halki en route to other islands but not returning the same day.

THE ISLAND

This barren, dry, rocky island which relies on drinking water shipped over from Rhodes, is a sanctuary of peace and an idyllic escape from reality. It is almost but not quite traffic free with the few hundred residents owning just a handful of cars between them but they are hardly racing around since there is virtually nowhere to go! The port town of **Nimborio** grew wealthy on sponge fishing around the turn of the 19th/20th century but later many of its sponge divers emigrated to the United States, to Tampron Springs in Florida, to set up a sponge diving community there. Fishing and sponge diving is still an important source of revenue for the island with tourism making a contribution.

Landing is made at Nimborio, the capital and now the only settlement on the island. Here colourfully shuttered imposing mansions crowd the water front and climb the hills behind watched over disinterestedly by derelict windmills. The sight of decaying mansions and the general air of neglect apparent a couple of decades ago has disappeared over recent years. Once designated the island of peace and friendship supported by UNESCO, money was provided for restoration which spurred islanders to return to rebuild their own crumbling mansions. An old problem, the lack of water, has proved a mixed blessing. Development has not exceeded the bounds of restoration whilst accommodation and services are sufficient to support a small amount of tourism. Now with a handful of tavernas and bars, and a beach nearby, Halki provides a relaxing place to unwind from the energy of modern life.

A short walk inland over the hill leads to a small sandy beach cradled in a small bay. A shady seat in the nearby taverna is the best place to watch bathers wading out far enough to swim.

Above: Halki harbour. *Below:* Halki

High above Nimborio, out of easy reach of pirates and close to the castle, is the now deserted village of **Horio** (Chorio). Sadly, the old mule trail up to Horio has been abandoned in favour of a modern paved road. It is the same road which passes the beach and heads off into the hills. Around 30-40 minutes of early morning walking along this exposed road is sufficient to reach the crest of the hill beneath the castle. Derelict houses are spread around but the interest here is focused on the **medieval castle of the Knights of St John**. Head left from the crest up the concrete path into a churchyard and go through the gate at the side to continue upwards. Some splendid sections of the castle walls remain and inside the derelict chapel still has some fine late Byzantine frescos. The views alone, of intricate coastlines and offshore islands, make the excursion worthwhile.

KARPATHOS

PRACTICAL DETAILS

Karpathos lies on an arc about half way between Rhodes and Crete. It is a fairly large island, the largest in the Dodecanese group after Rhodes, but under populated with only twelve villages housing some 5,000 inhabitants. Ferry boats connect Rhodes with Karpathos around twice a week but flights are much more frequent, with around four a day in summer. For visitors travelling via Athens, the most convenient programme is to include Karpathos either on the way to Rhodes or on the return journey. Travellers using the ferry service should be aware that the boats do not always run on windy days and schedules should be planned to accommodate this eventuality.

THE ISLAND

Karpathos is a long narrow island, effectively the summit region of a submerged mountain range, lying on a north-south axis. Most of the population lives in the south of the island but there is one remarkable village, Olympos, in the north which sits in isolation in its own time capsule, in an age long since past for the rest of Greece.

The island is not so easy to get around. A surfaced road links Karpathos Town (Pigadia) with the airport located on the extreme southern tip of the island and a surfaced road forms a southern circuit to take in the villages of Aperi, Volada, Othos, Piles, Finiki, Arkassa and Menetes. Villages further north are served by a track, most suited to four-wheeled drive vehicles, that penetrates the rugged, often cloud enshrouded mountains and leads all the way to Olympos.

Without industry and with little land suitable for cultivation, Karpathians have always been migrant workers and in recent years money sent home has made the island surprisingly prosperous. Since the completion of its international airport, Karpathos has turned more to tourism. One advantage of this late entry is that many of the hotels are of recent construction. Even more modest C class hotels offer a standard of comfort and service not always found in higher class hotels on other islands.

Karpathos Town, the capital, hustles around a port area in the southern corner of Vrondi Bay. Tourism has managed to capture the sea front area of this busy town and filled it imaginatively with tavernas, bars and restaurants, which is particularly picturesque under the evening lights. A few minutes walk to the north, is **Limniati** with its long stretch of sandy beach near where many hotels are located. This is probably the best base on the island although some may prefer **Ammoopi**, 8km (5miles) to the south which has three fine enclosed beaches but is somewhat isolated and supported only by hotels, apartments and tavernas.

The major excursion on the island is to the remote northern village of Olympos (Elymbos). It involves a boat journey to Diafani and a short bus journey up to the village itself. It is a highly packaged tour running daily but the most convenient way to enjoy Diafani and Olympos. The alternative is a lengthy drive along the spine of the island in a four wheeled vehicle.

Diafani, small and colourful, is the port area for Olympos. With more than a hundred beds in hotels and rooms, Diafani attracts its own measure of tourism and a programme of walks with drop down and pick up by boat is available.

Traditional costume is worn by many inhabitants, particularly by the women both here and in Olympos, for their normal daily routines. Married women wear black and single white with the single women and girls wearing more bright colours. Traditional footwear is the goatskin boot. Some of the village houses are in traditional style not dissimilar to those on Rhodes, featured on p.96, except the raised area for sleeping, here called the soufas, has an additional social function. When celebrations are held, such as family weddings or some religious occasion, the soufas is decorated with embroideries hung over the rails and transformed into the women's room where unmarried women sit and watch the celebrations taking place beneath on the floor of the house.

The journey by bus up to **Olympos** takes around 20 minutes and there are spectacular views just before arrival of the village perched on a ridge and spreading down the mountain side. The white houses, some flat roofed others with elements of neo-classical style, are clustered together allowing streets only wide enough for mules. Although it is not the first impression, there is considerable organisation in the village plan with rows of houses following contours along the hillside with higher and lower houses accessed by steps. Tavernas and snack bars are somehow squeezed into the village as well as a hotel and pensions. There is one picture postcard view not to be missed, the line of horseshoe-shaped windmills snaking out along a ridge just through the far end of the village. From here are spectacular views down the precipitous mountainside to the west coast.

Much of the interest in this village centres around the way of life and the customs still observed. The origins of the village are not clearly known but thought to be from around the 10th-15th century when shepherds and their families slowly gathered at one point or when the populace of a nearby village, Vroukounda, fled to the interior after destruction of their town by earthquake. Since then it has lived in virtual isolation and even its language is a unique dialect thought to maintain traces of ancient Doric and Phrygian languages. Inheritance laws are very strict and at no time are the fortunes of husband and wife ever combined but they are passed down undivided to the first born son and first born daughter. In this way, fortunes and personal power are preserved as well as some measure of population control. A second born has no inheritance, no land, no work, unless for other members of the family, and no prospects so is forced out to seek a fortune elsewhere.

The village church of **Koimisis Theotokou** (the Assumption of the Virgin Mary) has tiles on the floor which, until recently, belonged to certain women who had the privilege of standing there throughout the service. This tile was handed down to the eldest daughter in time. Those without tiles had to stand outside. More recently an annexe has been built where men and married women can sit whilst unmarried girls sit on the balcony above.

One food speciality to try before leaving the village is macarounes, not dissimilar to macaroni, flavoured with cheese.

Above & inset opposite: *Horseshoe-shaped windmills line the ridge at Olympos on Karpathos*

Additional Information

Symi

Telephone code 22410

Places to visit

Nautical Museum
Yialos
Open: 10.00am - 2.00pm every day
except Monday

Museum of Horio
Open: 10.00am - 2.00pm every day
except Monday

Halki

Places to visit

The medieval castle at Horio

Open site
Ferry Boats:

Daily service, except Sunday, departs
Halki 6.00am and returns from
Kamiros Skala at 2.30pm.

Sunday: departs Kamiros Skala at
9.00am and returns from Halki at
5.00pm.

Karpathos

Places to visit

Olympos

ACCOMMODATION

Hotels:

These are classified by the tourist authorities into De Luxe, AA and A class which are subject to a minimum price structure only. Bars, restaurants and swimming pools are the facilities that you expect to find but, on a cautionary note, the class in itself is not a guarantee of the standard of service. This island has some of the finest hotels in Greece with the likes of the Rodian Amathus Beach Hotel meeting the best international standards.These higher grade hotels are mostly found in the northern part of the island, especially Ixia, Rhodes Town and Faliraki, with newer ones north and south of Lindos.

In addition there are B, C and D classes for which maximum and minimum room rates are fixed by the tourist authority. These hotels are obliged to display their category and price behind the door of each room. There is no C in the Greek alphabet so this class is represented by the gamma sign 'Γ' Extra charges described as taxes or service may be added to the final rate and you need to check each time. Note that the charge is normally a room charge, not a charge per person and may or may not include breakfast. Room charges are seasonal with low, mid and high season rates. It is possible to bargain, especially for a stay of three days or more, but you are most likely to succeed when business is slack out of high season. Generally the C class hotels have rooms with bathrooms as do many of the D class but here it is not obligatory. Many of these hotels are often family run and offer a good level of cleanliness and comfort. The lower grade hotels may not have bar or restaurant facilities, except for breakfast. Air conditioning is becoming more widely introduced in the B and C class hotels and it is worth looking out for since high overnight temperatures throughout the summer months can make sleeping uncomfortable.

Pensions:

Accommodation of this kind in small hotels or private houses can also be very good. Again, the standards are controlled and graded by the tourist authorities but you really need to take each one on its own merit and do not hesitate to inspect before you commit yourself. At best they are very good with private bathroom facilities and a kindly Greek family to fuss over and take care of you. At worst you keep looking around!

Villas & Apartments:

There are many scattered around popular tourist locations with some resorts, like Faliraki, having more than others. Many are in the hands of letting agencies who place them with tour operators. One technique for searching them out is to read through the holiday brochures of companies who specialise in this type of accommodation. Many of these villas are often not in use until late May so, if you are around before then, it is possible to make private arrangements on the spot, sometimes at very attractive rates.

Rooms:

In the main tourist areas, there are generally plenty of private houses offering rooms. And, if you are looking for budget accommodation, some of these will be hard to beat. If you arrive on Rhodes by ferry, the chances are that you will be met at the dockside by a dancing cluster of assorted 'Room to let' notices, otherwise enquire at the local tourist office or with the Tourist Police who also help in these matters.

Web sites:

Two useful web sites for locating information and booking hotels on Rhodes are:
www.rodos.com and www.helios.gr/

BANKS

Opening hours are: Mon. - Thurs. 8.00am - 2.00pm, Friday 8.00am - 1.30pm. Early and late season some of the outlying banks close for the winter and it may be necessary to travel into Rhodes Town.

Cash dispensers are commonplace on Rhodes and it is easy to get cash just as you would at home. Use your same cash card, providing it bears a cirrus or maestro sign, and your usual pin number.

Visitors with Travellers Cheques and cash should have no trouble anytime. Most hotels offer exchange facilities and there are exchange bureaus in most resorts which stay open late into the night.

There is a bank and post office in Rhodes airport but these only open normal business hours. There are also cash dispensers.

Post Offices are open only on weekdays from 7.30am - 2.00pm. They are closed on Saturday and Sunday.

CLIMATE

Rhodes boasts one of the sunniest climates in Greece and from June to September the island experiences atmospheric stability with a succession of cloudless days. Temperatures rise regularly into the 30°s C and the heat is only tempered by the Meltemi wind which starts around May and blows from the north with persistent regularity. The north facing west coast takes the brunt of the wind and the east coast is more sheltered. In addition there is a daily cycle of wind throughout the summer with wind off the sea in the morning as the land heats up rapidly and the reverse after sunset when the land loses heat.

The monotonous pattern of endless days of sunshine and wind usually changes in September or sometimes a little later when depressions start to move west to east through the Mediterranean. Although the temperature falls, the weather remains warm and showers are possible and increasingly likely as autumn moves towards winter.

The cyclonic storms of winter arrive suddenly and the rain can be very heavy, up to 4in in a day causing flash floods off the mountains and filling the wide river beds. Winter continues as a mixture of heavy rain and periods of sunshine with January as the wettest month. Frost is rare and snow falls only in exceptionally hard winters.

According to the flowers, spring arrives early, as early as March but this month normally has a high number of days with rain. Spring here is as variable as anywhere in Europe. Some years March is a fine month with low rainfall, plenty of sunshine and comfortably high temperatures. In a late spring, rain showers, cool temperatures and cloudy skies persist until well into May when the transition to summer can then be almost immediate.

CRIME & THEFT

On an island like Rhodes which receives many thousands of visitors annually, some crime and theft is inevitable. There is no need to feel threatened in any way, even throughout the evening but it is sensible to be cautious late at night, especially women on their own. Rape and muggings, unfortunately do occur but not in the quiet country areas, as might be expected, but near to the high-life night spots like the main street in Faliraki.

Many hotels have safety deposit boxes available for guests at a small charge. Otherwise, keep valuables out of sight. This is particularly true if you have a car. Cameras, personal stereos and the like are best carried with you but if you need to leave them in the car make sure they are locked in the boot.

If you are unfortunate enough to suffer a loss through theft or carelessness then report it to the Lost and

Average Temperature

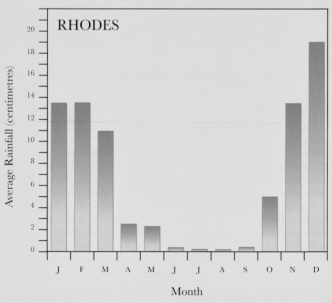

Found Office, Tel: 22410 23294, or the Tourist Police Tel 22410 27423. Multilingual police in this department wear a badge showing the languages spoken. There is a form to complete if an insurance claim is contemplated.

If your loss includes a passport then you will need to contact your Consul. See p.178.

CURRENCY & CREDIT CARDS

Greece was amongst the first twelve countries to replace their own national currency with the euro. Notes of legal tender have values of 500, 200, 100, 50, 20, 10 and 5 euros. One and two euro coins are available along with 50, 20,10, 5, 2 and 1 cent coins, although the cents are called lepta in Greece. The notes are identical in design in all countries of the eurozone but the coins have a national design on one side.

Travellers cheques and hard currencies are freely accepted at banks, Post Offices and Exchange Bureaus. Credit cards and charge cards are also widely accepted in hotels, shops and restaurants especially in Rhodes Town. While some of the larger petrol stations in town will accept credit cards, do not count on plastic to pay for petrol in the countryside.

Always take your passport when changing money. Even though the production of a passport may not be a necessary requirement, the Greeks rely on them as a means of identification. You may even be asked for it when purchasing an internal flight ticket. The cost of changing money in terms of commission does vary and it pays to check; normally the cheapest place is at a bank and the worst place is the hotel reception.

FACILITIES FOR THE DISABLED

Whilst there is an awareness of this problem, few practical steps have been taken to improve matters. As yet only the top hotels provide anything like adequate facilities. Outside Rhodes Town, very few places have pavements and where present they are high above the road. Presumably they are high to stop motorists parking on them. This creates a difficulty in making ramps since these descend so steeply they are more of a danger than a help.

DRIVING ON RHODES

Driving on Rhodes is on the right hand side of the road and overtaking on the left. In the event of an accident where the driver was proven to be on the wrong side of the road, the insurance is invalidated. Unless there are signs indicating otherwise, the speed limits are as follows: built-up areas 50kph (31mph), outside built-up areas 90kph (56mph).

Traffic moving along main roads outside towns has priority at intersections; in towns give way to traffic from the right. On approaching and on roundabouts, vehicles must give way to traffic coming from the right.

Greek law states that a car must also carry: a fire extinguisher, first aid kit and a warning triangle but these are not always found in hired vehicles. Children are not allowed to travel in a front seat.

The carrying of petrol in cans is forbidden as is the use of main beam headlights in towns and cities. Safety belts must be worn at all times and do not be dissuaded from this by the fact that many Greek motorists do not always use them. There are days when the police crack down hard on offenders. These occasions are usually well advertised but the news may escape you, especially if you are on the move. The same warning applies to motorcyclists. It is mandatory for driver and passenger to wear a crash helmet.

There are fixed penalties for certain motoring offences including illegal overtaking, going through a red light, driving without a seat belt, driving the wrong way down a one-way street, illegal parking and motor cyclists not wearing a helmet. The fines are mostly heavy and you will be told where to pay. The police are not empowered to collect fines on the spot.

Parking in Rhodes Town is something of a problem although there are large car parks on the front just north of the entrance to Mandraki harbour. These tend to fill early and often the best solution is to leave the car in the suburbs and walk.

There are parking meters in the blue zone central area of Rhodes town which are in operation from 9am -2pm and 4.30 -8.30pm weekdays with Saturdays 9am - 2pm. Sunday is free. These areas are marked by blue lines on the roadside. Yellow zones are for official services only and white zones are free.

Vehicular access to the old town is prohibited to non-residents.

With one of the worst accident rates in Europe, driving in Greece demands a cautious attitude from the onset. The discipline shown by the majority of drivers in western European countries, which brings order to traffic flow, is often missing from Greek drivers but the Rhodian drivers are a little more orderly. Drive with your own safety in mind. Another major hazard is the state of the roads. Pot holes are a serious danger and can be encountered unexpectedly even on well surfaced roads. Some of the holes are large enough to cause damage to tyres and wheels. A line of rocks on the road guiding you towards the centre is the usual warning of edge subsidence and there will often be no other warning signs. Minor roads, which are well surfaced, may suddenly become unmetalled. Road works may have no hazard warning signs or irregular ones such as a pile of earth or a milk crate with a small flag.

Motorists from EU countries need only a valid driving licence from their home country, others require an International Driving Licence.

Car hire:

Rhodes is expensive for car hire and a better deal can be arranged by booking and paying in advance of departure. The minimum age for car hire is 21, although many hire companies insist on 23, and 25 for jeeps and minibuses.

International car hire companies, such as Avis, Hertz, Europe Car, Budget and Eurodollar are well represented on Rhodes. In Britain, companies like Transhire (Tel 0870 789 8000 or www.transhire.com) offer rates including full insurance and unlimited mileage which are significantly lower than those available on the island. There are also many local companies but choose carefully and examine the rates most carefully. Normally, the advertised basic rate is limited to 100km daily and does not include CDW insurance. On top of all this is VAT at 18%.

Third party insurance is compulsory under Greek law and this cost will be added to the hire charge. An additional optional insurance is collision damage waiver (CDW) and it is imperative to take it. This cannot be stressed too strongly. Should you be unfortunate enough to be involved in an accident without CDW insurance and the costs cannot be recovered from a third party then the consequences can be frightening. At best you may be faced with a huge repair bill, at worst you could end up in jail until it is fully paid.

Tyres and damage to the underside of the car are mostly excluded from the insurance cover. Take time when you are accepting the car to inspect the tyres and, if not fully satisfied, do not accept the vehicle. It is worth a moment too to check that lights and indicators are fully operational. Before you drive away, make sure you have the agent's telephone number.

Check with the hire company if a car is to be taken on ferries. Your car insurance does not cover you for damage incurred whilst on board ship.

Motorcycles:

Above comments on insurance apply also to hiring a motorcycle or moped. There is a problem over crash helmets too. The law says very clearly that these must be worn and insist that they are provided or can be hired along with the bike. If you intend to hire a motorcycle, it is worth checking the fine print in the medical section of the holiday insurance taken out in your home country. Such is the concern over motorcycle accidents that some companies are specifically excluding medical care for injuries arising this way.

Breakdowns:

It is a legal requirement to place a warning triangle 100m/yds behind the car. Next step is to contact the car hire agency or if the car is private, contact Elpa by dialling 104. Elpa has reciprocal arrangements with European motoring organisations, like the British AA.

NEAREST FOREIGN EMBASSIES & CONSULATES ARE:

Australia
37 D Soutsou Street & An Tsocha
115 21 Athens
Tel 210 645 0404

Canada
4 I. Genadou Street
115 21 Athens
Tel 210 7273 400

New Zealand
24 Xenias
115 28 Athens
Tel 210 771 0112

USA
Embassy-Consulate
91 Vass. Sophias Avenue
115 21 Athens
Tel 210 721 2951

UK
Consulate
3 Pavlou Mela
Rhodes
Tel 22410 27306 & 27247

ELECTRICITY

Mains electricity is supplied at 220 volts AC. Electrical equipment should be fitted with a continental two pin plug or an appropriate adapter used. A wide selection of adapters for local plugs to interchange between two and three pin (not UK three pin) are available cheaply on the island.

GREEK TIME

Greek normal time is 2 hours ahead of GMT. The clocks advance one hour for summertime starting the last

Fact File

Road Signs

Fortunately, international road signs are used throughout the island but there may be occasions when you encounter temporary signs written in Greek.

Accidents and Legal Advice

In the event of an accident involving personal injury or damage to property, both the law and your insurance require that it is reported to the police. Start by contacting the Tourist Police by dialling (22410) 27423 and asking their advice.

ELPA (tel 104) offer free legal advice concerning Greek legislation on car accidents and insurance.

Fact File

Sunday in March and ending the last Sunday in October, in line with other EU countries.

America and Canada: Greek normal time is ahead of time in America, 7 hours ahead of Eastern Standard, 8 hours ahead of Central, 9 hours ahead of mountain and 10 hours ahead of Pacific Time.

Australia and New Zealand; Greek normal time is 7½ hours behind South Australia, 8 hours behind New South Wales, Tasmania and Victoria and 10 hours behind time in New Zealand. These differences relate to GMT but, to take into account clock changes for Daylight Saving hours, the following corrections should be made: add 1 hour to these differences from late September to the end of March and subtract 1 hour from late March to the end of September.

HEALTH CARE

For minor ailments like headaches, mosquito bites or tummy upsets, head for the chemist shop (farmakion). If you need a further supply of prescription drugs make sure to take a copy of your prescription and the chances are that you will be able to get them, and cheaply too.

Consular Help

Consular help is on hand in times of emergency but this is largely in an advisory capacity. The following comments are offered in terms of guidelines only and do not fully define the powers of the office. The Consul can:

help with problems over a lost passport and issue an emergency one if necessary;

help with problems over lost money or tickets but only by contacting relatives or friends at your request to ask them to provide the finance needed;

advise on the details of transferring funds;

encash a cheque supported by a valid banker's card but only in an emergency and as a last resort when there are no other options;

make a loan to cover repatriation expenses when this is the absolute last resort;

arrange for next of kin to be informed following an accident or death and advise on procedures;

act for nationals arrested or imprisoned to inform relatives;

give guidance on organisations experienced in tracing missing people;

provide a list of local interpreters, English speaking doctors and solicitors.

They do not involve themselves in finding work or obtaining work permits. Neither will they investigate a crime, give legal advice, instigate legal procedures on your behalf or attempt to interfere with the Greek legal procedures. Nationals in hospital or imprisoned can only expect the same treatment as the Greeks and the Consul has no power to gain better conditions.

Pharmacies are open normal shop hours and most seem to speak English. Certain chemist shops are on a rota to provide a 24 hour service and information for the nearest is posted in the pharmacy window.

If it is a doctor or dentist you require, the chemist shop should again be able to assist. If that does not work then contact the Tourist Police (tel 22410 274230. There are plenty of English speaking doctors and dentists on Rhodes.

Problems really start if hospital treatment is required. European countries have reciprocal arrangements with the Greeks for free medical treatment, subject to certain restrictions. For this reason British visitors should take an E111 form obtained from the Post Office. The story does not end there. To operate the scheme you need to find the local Greek Social Insurance office (IKA) who, after inspecting your E111, will direct you to a registered doctor or dentist. If you are in a region remote from the IKA office, which is in Rhodes Town, then you must pay privately for your treatment and present your bills to an IKA official before you leave Rhodes. Up to half your costs may be refunded. The best answer is to ensure that you have adequate holiday insurance cover and an E111.

Emergency treatment, sunburn, broken bones etc., is free in state hospitals. The situation is less happy if you require treatment as an in patient. In many of these hospitals, nursing care is restricted only to medical treatment and it is left to the family to supply general nursing care, drinks, food and even blankets.

It is generally preferable to activate private medical insurance.

Health hazards:

Some of the more obvious ones can be avoided with a little care. Sunburn and sunstroke fall into this category. The sun is very burning even on a hazy day, particularly on Rhodes, so great care is needed in protecting yourself, especially at the start of your holiday. Crawling beneath a parasol is not necessarily the full answer since the sun's rays reflect to some extent from the sand. Avoid, if possible, sunbathing in the middle of the day, from 10am until around 2.00pm when the sun it at its highest and most direct. Sun creams help considerably but, at least for the first few days, take some very light clothing to cover up and control the exposure of your skin to the sun. A slowly acquired tan lasts longer.

Even mild sunburn can be painful and may cause a chill feeling but if fever, vomiting or blistering occurs then professional help is essential.

Mosquitoes feed most actively at dusk and dawn but they can still be a nuisance throughout the evening and the night. If you sit or dine outside in the evening, particularly near trees, either cover up your arms and legs or use insect repellent. If you happen to be dining when bitten and have either lemon or vinegar to hand, both of these are effective treatments which quickly relieve symptoms. An electric machine which slowly vaporises a pellet is very efficient, especially in a closed room and there are sprays available for more instant results if intruders are spotted. Anthisan cream is an effective treatment for bites, particularly if applied immediately.

Care is needed on the beach to avoid stings from jelly fish and, in rocky regions, from sea urchins. If you are unlucky enough to have a brush with the latter then it is important to ensure that all the spines are properly removed. Wearing beach shoes will give your feet some protection from stings of this nature.

Stomach upsets are perhaps the most common ailment. The excess olive oil used in cooking and over salads can be a cause of this so take care with oily foods, at least to start with. The digestive system adjusts to this within a few days and you can soon eat giant beans swimming in oil without fear. Squeeze plenty of fresh lemon over your food to counter the oil and, if still troubled, an acidic drink, like Coca-Cola, helps to settle things. Drinking wine to excess can cause similar symptoms too. More serious are the upsets caused by bad water and bad food. Generally the water on Rhodes is safe to drink but in high summer it pays to be more careful and use bottled water which is freely available. Avoiding food poisoning is not always possible but there are elementary precautions that can help. Most tavernas prepare cooked dishes for the lunch time trade and these are left keeping warm until finally sold. If they are still there in the evening, and they often are, avoid them. Ask for something which will require grilling or roasting.

Holiday insurance:

Whichever holiday insurance you choose, make sure that the cover for medical expenses is more than adequate. It helps too if there is an emergency 24 hour contact to take care of arrangements, including repatriation if necessary. Injuries caused whilst taking part in certain hazardous pursuits are normally excluded from medical cover. Look carefully at the specified hazardous pursuits; in recent times, injuries caused by riding a moped or motorbike have been added to the list by some insurers.

LANGUAGE

Many Greeks speak good English, especially in tourist areas. Children learn it in state schools and most of them attend private schools as well. After all, English is the official second language in Greece and all official notices are presented in Greek and English, at least the more recent notices. Therein lies the danger. It is all too easy to expect and rely on every Greek to speak English which is clearly not the case when you move into country areas.

Some knowledge of the Greek language is not only useful to help you get by, but can enhance enormously the pleasure of your holiday. The Rhodians really warm to you if you make the slightest effort with their language. Do not worry about perfection in pronunciation in the beginning, just give it a go. The Greeks are very outgoing and, if they have any English, they will try it out no matter how fractured it is. Take a leaf from their book. As long as you make an effort, the Greeks will love you for it and once you can string a few words together you might find their hospitality overwhelming.

Perhaps the biggest hurdle to getting started is the Greek alphabet itself. If you take a little time to study it, you will find it is not really so different. Isolate the letters which are unique to the Greek alphabet and the remainder generally follow the sequence of the English alphabet. The language is phonetic so time taken over learning the sounds of the letters will be well rewarded in subsequent progress. Two pieces of advice to get you started on the right foot. (1) Treat all vowels equally and do not attempt to lengthen them. (2) Avoid breaking a word down into syllables as in English, instead, follow the stress pattern indicated by the accent in the word. Arm yourself with a good phrase book and give it a try!

PLACE NAMES

With no official transliteration, the latinisation of the Greek alphabet is open to various interpretations which leads to much confusion. The conversion of the double consonants, for example, is one cause of difficulty. The Greek nt is pronounced as d at the start of a word but nd in the middle. A Greek word starting with nt is almost invariably Latinised to begin with d but in the middle of the word both nt and nd can be observed. Afandou on Rhodes appears on some maps as Afantou. Vowel sounds, especially e and i, do not always strictly correspond so there is a tendency to substitute the more phonetically correct. Some single consonants have no strict equivalent either, such as X, pronounced as the ch in loch, and this is Latinised to ch, which is a mile away phonetically, or h which is a little better. The village of Xora appears as Chora or Hora. All these difficulties are reflected in the spelling of place names. Pick up three different maps and it is more than likely that many of the same villages will have three different spellings. The philosophy adopted for this book is firstly to follow the spelling observed on the sign outside the village or use the spelling which leads to a more accurate pronunciation. With a number of Greek islands, the English name is not the same as the Greek name and may bear no relationship, Corfu, for example is the English name for Kerkyra. With Rhodes the difference is not so marked but the Rhodians like to hear their name, Rodos, used where possible.

LUGGAGE

Since Greece is a full member of the EU, it is very likely that, should you forget your favourite brand of toothpaste, you will be able to buy it in the shops there. All leading brands of food and products are freely available, give or take some national peculiarities. Brands of tea and breakfast cereal fall into this category. The Greeks do not normally start the day with breakfast instead they nibble the morning away with their own versions of fast food, cheese pies (tiropitta) and souvlaki in pitta bread are well favoured. However, a limited range of breakfast cereals can be bought in most tourist regions. With tea it is a little easier, if you have a favourite brand of tea or tea bags then it is easy to find room for some in your luggage.

There are a few other items which are worth considering if only to save time shopping when you are there.

A universal sink plug - not so essential but always worth having when travelling.

An electric mosquito repeller and tablets - these are readily available in Greece but small 'travel' types are freely available which are a convenient size for packing and will last for years. Make sure you buy one with a continental 2 pin plug.

Insect repellent - if you prefer a particular brand, buy it at home.

Two other useful items are a compact folding umbrella, particularly if you are visiting Rhodes outside the main season. Rain showers tend to be short and, with the rain falling straight down, an umbrella gives good protection, better than a waterproof which can quickly make you hot and sweaty. A small rucksack is useful too, not just for if you go walking, but for general use when heading for the beach or off on a shopping trip. Walkers might consider taking a plastic water bottle. It is important to carry water when walking in a hot climate and it is difficult to buy a plastic bottle in Greece which does not leak into your rucksack! The same advice is offered to motorists too. Unless you live in a hot climate, it is sometimes hard to appreciate the constant need to drink and how that need is best supplied by nothing other than water. Simply having water on hand when needed can add a lot to your comfort level and enjoyment of the excursion.

It is rarely necessary to take a heavy jumper but it is always useful to take some thinner layers of clothing which you can wear together. Sometimes it is cool in the evening or you may feel cool after the heat of the sun. If you intend to do any serious walking, walking on country tracks as opposed to city streets, make sure you have suitable footwear.

Most basic medical requirements, plasters, bandages, headache pills can be bought in chemist shops on Rhodes. More than that, many drugs normally available in Britain only on prescription can be bought over the counter on demand and at reasonable prices.

Note that codeine and drugs

Fact File

containing codeine are strictly banned in Greece so be sure to exclude these from your luggage.

MAPS

In recent years, Road Editions has produced a range of excellent maps for most parts of Greece including many islands. The map for Rhodes is no. 202 produced in a scale of 1:100,000. No other map of Rhodes currently available has the same accuracy. Generally, the signposting is fairly good on the island with the Greek signs displayed first with the Latinised version a little nearer the junction.

NEWSPAPERS & MAGAZINES

The Financial Times, most British newspapers, a selection from European countries and the Herald Tribune are usually available in Rhodes Town and centres of tourism. Mostly they are one day late and sometimes more. Expect a fair mark up in price. The place to look for newspapers is in the tourist shops, supermarkets and at the kiosks (periptera) where you will see them displayed on racks or along the counter.

Also available in Rhodes Town on the day of issue is Athens News, published in the English language. It contains a mix of local and international stories but the entertainment section announcing events and concerts relates only to Athens. It gives an interesting insight into Greek attitudes to current events. By far the best local paper, and free, is the Rodos News. Focused clearly on the island, it is packed with useful information on local events, history, news and travel timetables. Look for it in the Tourist Office and many other shops on the island, especially travel agents.

PASSPORTS & VISAS

UK nationals require a passport to enter Greece.

Nationals from America, Australia, Canada, New Zealand, Norway, Sweden, Finland and certain other nations require only a valid passport for a stay of up to 3 months in Greece.

Visitors will also need to produce a passport when registering at a hotel.

PETS

Cats and dogs require health and rabies inoculation certificates issued by a veterinary authority in the country of origin not more than 12months (cats 6 months) and not less than 6 days prior to arrival.

PHOTOGRAPHY

Signs which show a picture of a camera crossed out indicate a prohibited area for photography. Notices of this kind are posted near every military establishment, no matter how small or insignificant. Disregard this at your peril. The Greeks are still paranoid about security and anyone found using a camera in a prohibited zone faces unpleasant consequences. The photographer is normally held in custody whilst the film is developed and inspected. It could mean overnight detention.

Photography on archaeological sites is free but if you wish to use a tripod without the insertion of a live subject then a fee is demanded.

Photography with a camera mounted on a tripod is prohibited in museums as is the use of flash in some. Video cameras are often subject to a fee.

Outdoors, the light for photography is brilliant. Summer haze can cause difficulties with distant shots but the use of a UV or Skylight filter is helpful here. Some of the clearest days occur in spring when a cool north wind blows. Midday light is harsh and contrasty, mornings and evening provide the best lighting conditions for serious photography.

PLACES TO VISIT

Ancient Sites & Monasteries

Most of the ancient sites are fenced off and there is an entrance fee to look around. Generally they are free to all on Sunday in winter and closed on Monday. Opening and closing times have been regularised and these can be found either in the text or at the end of the appropriate chapter. Monasteries are often closed in the afternoon so, as a general guide, it is best to plan a morning visit. Do not count on being able to buy site guides at all sites, sometimes only glossy books are sold. If your interest runs deeper than the information given in the chapters of this book, the best advice is to go equipped with your own guide.

Students can claim reduced fees on production of a student's card.

Archaeological sites are closed on certain public holidays which include January 1st, March 25th, Good Friday and Easter Monday, May 1st and December 25th and 26th.

Museums

Here again there is a charge for admission and all close on a Monday. Refer to the end of the appropriate chapter for further details.

The museums too are closed, or open only for a short while, on the public holidays listed under ancient sites. In addition they have half-days on Shrove Monday, Whitsunday, August 15th, October 28th and Epiphany, January 6th.

NUDISM

Topless bathing is commonplace on all public beaches on Rhodes. Nude bathing is not acceptable on public beaches but is practised with discretion on some of the more remote and secluded beaches although these are increasingly difficult to find.

POSTAL SERVICES

Post Offices open on weekdays from 7.30am - 2pm. They are closed on Saturday and Sunday.

Stamps (grammatosima) can be purchased at the post office, sometimes at a special counter, or at a kiosk (periptero). They are also available in many shops and some of the larger hotels but at a slightly increased price.

Letters from Greece to overseas destinations are delivered fairly speedily, 4/6 days for Europe, 6/8 for America and longer for Australia and New Zealand. For a speedier delivery, ask for express post on which there is a fairly modest surcharge but it cuts 2/3 days off the delivery time.

Postcards take forever, or so it seems, especially at peak holiday times. Even to nearby Europe they regularly take two weeks which often means you have reached home before the cards you sent. Cards go at the same postal rate as letters so one technique is to slip a card inside an airmail envelope and have it treated as a letter. It leaves more space on the card for writing too. Envelopes (fakellos) can be bought very cheaply at stationers.

Anyone staying long enough to receive mail can use Poste Restante. This system works fairly well in Rhodes Town. The letter should be clearly addressed and marked Poste Restante; be sure that your name is clearly printed. Some identification will be required, usually passport, when you collect your letter. Letters are held for one month.

Postcodes on the island vary with the town. Some of the major resorts

Fact File

Fact File

are listed below:

Rhodes Town	851 00
Ixia & Trianda	851 01
Faliraki	851 02
Lindos	851 07

PUBLIC HOLIDAYS & FESTIVALS

The Greek calendar overflows with red letter days; public holidays, Saints days and festivals. On public holidays, banks, shops and offices are closed although restaurants and tavernas normally stay open. Public transport is often interrupted too, reverting either to a Sunday service or to none at all. Petrol stations also close for many of the holidays. The days to watch out for are:

1st January - New Year's Day
6th January - Epiphany
7th March - Rhodes Independence Day
25th March - Greek Independence Day
Monday before Lent - Clean Monday
April - Good Friday & Easter Monday
1st May - May Day
15th August - Assumption of the Blessed Virgin Mary
28th October - 'Ochi' Day
25th December - Christmas Day
26th December - Boxing Day

Easter is variable and does not always coincide with Easter throughout the rest of Europe.

Name-days are one reason why the calendar is so full of celebrations. It has been a long tradition for Greeks to ignore birthdays to celebrate instead the special day of their saint, and there are a lot of saints. If you see people wandering around with cake boxes neatly tied with fancy ribbon, or bunches of flowers or unusual activity around one of the many churches, then the chances are that it is a name day. The custom is for the person celebrating to offer hospitality to friends, to neighbours and to almost anyone who will partake of a little ouzo and refreshments.

Some of the big name days to watch out for are:

23rd April - St. George's day; all Georges everywhere celebrate their special day but in addition it is also the national day of Greece.

21st May - Saints Konstantinos and Eleni.

29th June - St. Peter and St Paul

15th August - Assumption of the Blessed Virgin Mary. The is the day when millions of Marias celebrate and an important day in the religious calendar often marked by local pilgrimages or festivals.

8th November - for all Michaels and Gabriels.

6th December - the feast of St. Nicholas.

Easter is the biggest and the most important celebration of the year. The arrival of Carnival time starts the long build up. This festival takes place throughout the three weeks before Lent and may commence as early as late January. Fancy dress is an important part of the tradition throughout the whole of Greece. It arises from the period of Turkish occupation when the Greeks were banned from conducting these celebrations. Driven under cover, festivities continued with people disguised to prevent recognition. Now it is firmly rooted into the custom and fancy dress and costumes are worn at all events. The children wander the streets in fancy dress and traditionally show defiance by wearing their disguises on the last school day of Carnival.

All this comes to an abrupt end with a complete change of mood on 'Clean Monday' (Kathari Deutera), the Monday before Lent. This is a public holiday when families traditionally exodus to the country to fly kites and to picnic, which mostly means heading to a taverna. Special meat-free menus are the order of the day.

It is back to the quiet life throughout Lent which is still strictly observed by many, especially in country regions. Serious preparations for

Easter start on Maundy Thursday. How hens are persuaded to lay so actively for the occasion remains a mystery but shoppers are out buying eggs, not by the tens but by the hundreds. The rest of the day is spent in boiling the eggs and dying them red in the process. The colour red is supposed to have protective powers and the first egg dyed belongs to the Virgin.

Good Friday is a day of complete fast and widely observed. In tourist regions tavernas are open and life goes on as normal but in country areas it can be difficult or impossible to find food. Yellow or brown 'impure' candles are on sale everywhere ready for the evening church service. The sombre mood of the day is heightened by the continual tolling of church bells. It is a day for remembering their own dead; graves are visited and wreaths are laid. In the evening, the burial of Christ is the most moving and widely attended service in the whole of the Greek Orthodox calendar. The Epitaphios, the funeral bier of Christ, is centre stage in the services which start around 9 o'clock in the evening. Garlanded with fresh flowers and with a gilded canopy, the Epitaphios bearing the coffin of Christ is ceremoniously taken from church in dignified candle-lit procession followed by silent mourners. The processions from all the local churches meet in the town square for a further short service. This is the most poignant moment of the evening, cafés close, tavernas close and there is not one Greek who would willingly miss it. The processions return slowly to their churches, stopping at each street corner for a short prayer.

Saturday brings an air of expectancy. Gone are the yellow candles; white candles are being eagerly bought ready for the evening service. Funereal drapes are removed in the churches and decorations of laurel and myrtle take their place. In dimly lit churches everywhere, services begin. Slowly the light intensity increases reaching full brightness at midnight when priests triumphantly chant 'Christ is risen' (Christos anesti). The sanctuary doors open to show that the Epitaphios is empty. Light from the priest's candle is passed to the congregation and that flame is rapidly passed from candle to candle until it reaches the waiting crowds outside. Fire crackers drown the clamour of the church bells as the crowd erupts in joyous celebration and greetings of 'Christos anesti' ring out loudest of all. The crowds disperse shortly carefully protecting their burning candle; it is a good omen to enter the home with the flame still burning and make a sooty sign of the cross on the door lintel.

Sunday is a day of out and out rejoicing. The big occasion of the day is roasting the lamb or goat. On Rhodes oven roasting is traditional but spit roasting is also popular. Charcoal fires are lit early in the morning and the spit roasting is done with loving care over some 5 hours with copious quantities of ouzo or retsina to help things along. All those red eggs now appear and are used in friendly competition. Each contestant taps their egg hard enough to break an opponent's but not their own.

Easter Monday has no special ceremonies or rituals and passes as any normal public holiday.

CULTURAL EVENTS

In addition to the major festivals listed with each chapter, religious fairs, *panayiria*, are commonplace in the summer months. Panayiria are a celebration of the name day of a particular church or monastery and usually held in the vicinity of the establishment. Celebrations are colourful, often beginning on the eve of the name day and continue throughout the actual day. Eating, drinking and dancing are central to any celebration for the Greeks so the barbecue is certain to be in operation. When the crowds are big enough, the vendors join in selling just about anything, baubles, bangles and

Fact File

beads.

A word of warning too. Each town and village has its own saint's day and sometimes, depending on the local whim and the phase of the moon, a holiday is called. This decision is often not taken until the day before so there is no way you can plan for such eventualities.

PUBLIC TOILETS

The most usual sign is WC with figures to indicate ladies (gynaikon) and gents (andron). Toilets in Rhodes Town are surprisingly good and usually free, certainly above the standard normally found in Greece. There are also toilets in museums and at archaeological sites which are also good. Toilet paper is sometimes supplied where there is an attendant and very occasionally elsewhere. Take your own supply.

PUBLIC TRANSPORT

Buses

There is a good and fairly frequent bus service in operation serving towns and villages on both sides of the island. Buses serving the eastern side of the island start from Rimini Square (outside the Sound and Light Theatre) and those serving the western side from the bus station in Averof Street (adjoining new market). Printed timetables are usually available from the Tourist Office and are included in the Rodos News free paper. The frequency of services is much less in winter but builds up as the tourist season gets underway. Throughout May the timetable changes weekly until the service reaches its maximum frequency sometime in June which is then held until early September. The timetable holds equally from Monday through to Saturday but Sunday sees a reduction in the number of buses to about half.

The buses depart Rhodes Town strictly on schedule and sometimes a

fraction early. Intermediate times depend on traffic conditions but on quieter days, particularly Sundays, it pays to be at the stop early.

Buses from East Side serve the following destinations: Faliraki, Kalithies, Lindos, Kolimbia, Afandou, Archangelos, Haraki, and Lardos and intermediate destinations *en route*.

The West side station has a frequent service, virtually half hourly all day long, to the airport which is also convenient for Ixia, Trianda and Paradission.

There are also local town buses which run half hourly and connect Rhodes Town with its close suburbs. These start from Mandraki harbour and a fixed price ticket must be purchased from the ticket office by the bus station before boarding. Two of the buses in particular are useful to visitors, the CT3 to Rodini Park and the CT5 to Monte Smith.

Taxis

Taxis are relatively cheap and well used on Rhodes. All licensed taxis are designated by a roof sign and fitted with a meter which displays the fare in euros. The rate of charges and surcharges are all fixed. Within the city boundaries taxi fares are charged at the single rate and you may see 1 displayed in a solitary box on the meter. Once you travel outside the city boundary, the double rate applies so it is likely you will see the driver alter the meter so that 2 shows in the box. Legitimate small surcharges are allowed for a sizeable piece of luggage, for attending an airport, port or station for the benefit of passengers, and for late night or very early morning travel. Surcharges are permitted too at holiday times, especially Christmas and Easter. Picking up a second fare is allowed too so you may find yourself sharing a taxi.

There is a list of official taxi fares posted near the main taxi stand in Rhodes town and elsewhere on the island. It is also reproduced in the Rodos News and available from the tourist office.

If you intend to travel on a journey where the fare is not displayed, it is common practice to negotiate your fare with the driver before you start the journey. Do not hesitate to ask two or three drivers for a quote on the fare, it is the only yardstick available.

Most of the licensed taxi drivers are good and honest but there are always a few around who regard tourists as a good source of revenue. Some of the tricks encountered include; the meter does not work, the meter set on the double rate when it should be single and, worst of all, multiplying the charge by ten which is easily done by wrongly reading the display on the modern digital meter.

Radio Taxis (Tel 22410 64712) offer a 24 hour service island-wide otherwise, there are taxi ranks in most major resorts.

As usual, if there are no taxis at the rank the telephone will be unanswered. One last word of warning, taxis are sometimes scarce on Sundays, Bank, Public and religious holidays.

SHOPPING

Regulations on opening hours were relaxed some years ago to adjust to market needs. Different regions have their own views on this so there is now greater confusion than ever over opening times. Big supermarkets and department stores open: Monday - Friday   8.00am - 8.00pm. Saturday 8.00am - 3.00pm.

Shops and pharmacies: Monday & Wednesday 8.00am - 2.00pm. Tues., Thurs., & Fri. 8.00am - 2.00pm & 5.00pm - 8.00pm

There is also a duty rosta for pharmacies so that at least one in the vicinity is open on Saturday and Sunday. Usually a note on the door of the pharmacy details the duty chemist.

The opening hours for pharmacies are fairly typical of the opening hours in small towns and villages. They argue, with some justification, every-body wants to sleep in the afternoon and nobody wants to shop.

In tourist areas, shopping hours are much more relaxed. Tourist shops in particular are open all day long but supermarkets, butchers, bakers and the like tend to observe more restricted hours.

The periptero, the cornerstone of Greek society, is open all day long and from there you can buy anything from chocolate to ice creams, soap to postage stamps and road maps to matches.

SPORTS & PASTIMES

Water sports

Water sports are hugely popular on the island and virtually every resort provides some facilities.

Rhodes is an excellent island for wind surfers and one of the best locations in the Mediterranean. Many of the small bays and coves are ideally suited to this sport and boards can be hired in most holiday resorts. Favoured spots for the experts are the west coast, Ialyssos bay with its constant wind in summer, and down at Prasonissi at the southern tip of the island. Lessons for beginners are generally available too at rates which are still very reasonable.

Water-skiing is available at many of the larger resorts, especially on the east coast, as well as parascending.

Scuba diving is strictly prohibited unless in the control of a recognised diving school and the only location is Kallithea. With so many antiquities in the waters around Rhodes, it is forbidden to remove anything from the sea bed and infringements normally result in a prison sentence.

Ladiko is popular for snorkelling as is the adjacent Anthony Quinn bay.

Tennis

Courts are mostly to be found in the better class hotels but some allow non residents to use the facilities for a charge.

Golf

The 18 hole course at Afandou is the one and only course on the island.

Horse-riding

Horse riding for beginners and experts is possible with the Riding Club of Rhodes. Free transport to the stables near Asgourou is provided.

Walking

Rhodes provides abundant opportunities for hill and coastal walking and the 'Landscapes of Rhodes' published by Sunflower Books is a useful guide. There are a number of walks detailed throughout the pages of this book which might be enough for most visitors.

Yachting

Rhodes, a port of entry, is ideally positioned for those who wish to explore the area by sea and has a well equipped modern marina at Mandraki harbour. There is no size limit on boats and the facilities available include electricity, water, repairs, 40 ton hoist, slipway, diesel and petrol gardiennage and chandlery. Mooring fees are available on application. Entrance to the harbour can be dangerous in strong east to south-east winds. British Admiralty charts are available from Contact Yacht Agency who also hire out craft, crewed or bareboat, sail or power (Tel 22410 22927).

TELEPHONE SERVICES

Most telephone booths on the island have now been converted to card phones and these too are convenient and economical. Cards, loaded with 100 units, are available often from the shop or periptero nearest the booth.

It may be possible to use your own personal mobile but check before departure to see if your particular agreement allows you to roam.

Hotels have telephones for use by residents, mostly in the rooms but sometimes at reception. They charge a much higher rate per unit so it pays to ascertain the hotel rate and compare with phone card rates.

International dialling codes from Greece are as follows: UK & Northern Ireland 0044: United States & Canada 001: Australia 0061: New Zealand: 0064.

The exchange numbers for Rhodes cover three sectors. The north (22410) covers Rhodes Town roughly down to a line across between Soroni and Afandou. The south-west (22460) covering Embonas, Salakos, Monolithos and Apolakia and the south-east (22440) for Archangelos, Lindos, Lardos, Gennadi and Katavia.

TIPPING

There are no hard and fast rules on tipping. Normally, the Greeks simply leave behind the small change after a meal and perhaps the best guide is to reward only for good service in a restaurant. Taxi drivers expect a tip as does the chamber maid in the hotel otherwise it is entirely by discretion.

TRAVELLING TO RHODES

By Air

The easiest, cheapest and quickest way is to take a charter flight from Britain directly to the island. If travelling out of season or from America or Canada, the route is via Athens which may or may not require an overnight stop depending on arrival times. Olympic Airways handles the ongoing flights between Athens and Rhodes and it is usually possible to book this flight at the same time as the main flight. Aegean Airlines also offer internal flights from Athens to Rhodes. The International Airport on Rhodes lies on the west coast just south of Rhodes town.

Athens has a new International Airport, Eleftherios Venizelos, which opened in March 2001. Unfortunately, it is around 17.5 miles (28km) from Athens centre so travellers faced with an overnight stop will have a choice of the airport hotel or travelling into the city.

TRAVELLING FROM RHODES

By Boat

Rhodes is well connected by ferry to both Athens via the port of Piraeus and to other islands including Astypalea, Crete (Heraklion, Sitia and Ag Nikolaos), Folegandros, Halki, Kalymnos, Karpathos, Kassos, Kastelorizo, Kos, Leros, Lipsi, Milos, Nissyros Paros, Patmos, Santorini, Sifnos, Symi, Syros, Tilos.
   In addition to the ferries, there are now good hydrofoil services offering shorter journey times to many of the Dodecanese islands. Services start to operate in May and provide a full programme by June. Islands served include Halki, Symi, Tilos, Kos. Onward services from Kos link up with Kalimnos, Leros, Patmos, Agathonissi, Samos, Chios, Mitilini and to Alexandroupolis and Kavala on the mainland.

Excursion Boats

There are daily excursion boats running to Symi and to Turkey (Marmaris) from Rhodes Town throughout summer. Hydrofoils also operate excursions to Turkey.
   There is also a daily boat to Halki but only from Kamiros Skala.

Fact File

TOURIST INFORMATION CENTRES

   Greek National Tourist Organisation,
5, Archbishop Makariou & Papagou Streets, Rhodes, Greece.
Tel: (22410) 23255/21921/35226
Open: Mon-Fri 8.00am -2.00pm
Rhodes Town Information Office, Rimini Square/Mandraki.
Tel: (22410) 35945
Open daily (high season only): 8.00am - 9.00pm

USEFUL AND EMERGENCY TELEPHONE NUMBERS

(Rhodes Town Code 22410)
Police & Emergency services 100
Greek National Tourist Tel: 23255 & 21921
Tourist Police - Tel: 27423
Road assistance (ELPA) - Tel: 104
Airport Tel: 88700
Emergency 166 (can be dialled from any card phone with a card)
First Aid & Ambulance 22410 80000

Index

Published in the UK by
Landmark Publishing Ltd,
Ashbourne Hall, Cokayne Ave, Ashbourne, Derbyshire DE6 1EJ England
Tel: (01335) 347349 Fax: (01335) 347303 e-mail: sales@landmarkpublishing.co.uk
website: www.landmarkpublishing.co.uk

2nd Edition 2005
ISBN: 1 84306 121 X

Print: Gutenberg Press Ltd, Malta
Design: Simon Hartshorne
Editor: Kay Coulson

Front cover: Haraki beach
Back cover, top: Halki
Back cover, bottom: Agathi beach

Acknowledgements

Following our frequently disappointing experiences with tourist offices, it was refreshing to find Maria Thymianou in the Tourist Office in Rhodes town so well organised with information and so helpful. We thank her for all her help.

We would also like to thank Argo Holidays for help with accommodation in Faliraki and, in particular, we would like to thank the Rodian Amathus Hotel for their kind hospitality. It was an excellent experience and we were delighted with the overwhelming hospitality of the management and the friendliness of the staff. A special thank you must go to Nikos Stergiopoulos and Stefanos Karasiotos.

There is an input of information from many people when assembling a book such as this and to all those people we say thank you.